D1611423

WITHDRAWN

Kipling
&
Conrad

Kipling
&
Conrad

THE COLONIAL FICTION

John A. McClure

Harvard University Press

Cambridge, Massachusetts
and London, England
1981

Publication of this book has been aided by a
grant from the Andrew W. Mellon Foundation

Library of Congress Cataloging in Publication Data

McClure, John A., 1945–
    Kipling and Conrad, the colonial fiction.

    Includes bibliographical references and index.
    1. English fiction—History and criticism.
2. Colonies in literature.   3. Imperialism in
literature.   4. Kipling, Rudyard, 1865–1936—
Criticism and interpretation.   5. Conrad, Joseph,
1857–1924—Criticism and interpretation.   I. Title.
PR830.C6M38   823'.8'09358   81–4117
ISBN 0–674–50529–8   AACR2

To my parents

ACKNOWLEDGMENTS

I want to express my thanks first of all to Thomas Moser, Ian Watt, and Albert Guerard. I had the good fortune to begin my study of Conrad under their guidance at Stanford, and their instruction, criticism, and encouragement have been invaluable.

I am indebted as well to a number of friends — Rita Gentry, Sandra Drake, Hunt Hawkins, and Roger Harm — who share an experience of Africa and an interest in the literature of empire. For some ten years now we have stimulated, educated, and sustained each other in this interest, and my study is an expression of our collective effort.

Finally, I would like to thank my colleagues at University College, Rutgers, whose support and encouragement enabled me to complete this study.

CONTENTS

INTRODUCTION

"Mr. Conrad has in this book introduced us to the British merchant seaman, as Rudyard Kipling introduced us to the British soldier"—so wrote a reviewer of *The Nigger of the "Narcissus"* in 1898.[1] David Thorburn, citing this passage in a more recent study of Joseph Conrad, suggests that it offers "a just description of one of Conrad's fundamental ambitions as a writer" and is "high praise."[2] It seems to me that Thorburn is right both in ascribing this ambition to Conrad and in valuing its fulfillment. Certainly Conrad prided himself on introducing another social exotic, the colonialist, to the metropolitan reader. In *Heart of Darkness* he calls attention to this achievement by having Marlow's physician observe rather wistfully that "it would be . . . interesting for science to watch the mental changes of individuals, on the spot" in the Congo—interesting, but far too dangerous.[3] The doctor's expression of interest and unwillingness is an oblique advertisement for *Heart of Darkness* itself, and may remind the reader that the work's author has apparently done what the doctor feared to do. He has risked himself in dangerous regions to introduce us to the interesting beings who live there. George Orwell credits Rudyard Kipling with a similar achievement. Kipling's work, he observes, is the "only literary picture that we possess of nineteenth-century Anglo-India," because Kipling was the only literary man "coarse enough to be able to exist and keep his mouth shut in clubs and regimental messes."[4]

It has long been considered one of the functions of a certain kind of literature to enable us—the mostly middle-class readers of serious

fiction—to get to know people who live so far above or below us
that we will never be admitted to their company, or so far away in
time or space that we cannot hope to visit them, even if we would.
Literature also enables us to explore extreme experiences that fascin-
ate and frighten us and from which we draw back in real life. As a
writer's reputation grows, however, both he and his interpreters
are likely to deemphasize this aspect of his work, stressing instead
its aesthetic felicities and its elucidation of more perennial mysteries.
There are grounds, of course, for such a shift of focus; while an
author's contribution to ongoing philosophical discussions and his
elaboration of new modes of expression are likely to be of enduring
interest, especially to the student of literature, the images of life
that first win the public's attention by their novelty are likely to
grow familiar with time and so to lose their power of attraction.
Thus a certain shift of critical attention seems necessary if the work
is to endure.

In many instances, however, the tendency to ignore a writer's accomplishments as a chronicler of a particular social reality ends by
obscuring these accomplishments entirely and making his fiction
less enjoyable. The more unfamiliar the realms the author explores,
the more likely it is that this process will take place; public interest
in such realms tends to be intense but fleeting, and as they slip out
of the limelight they become unknown again without regaining the
glamor they once had. Thus the colonial struggles that Kipling and
Conrad portray may now appear, at least from a Eurocentric
perspective and in the light of the demise of colonialism, to be of
secondary importance. Thus history itself has conspired with the
writers and their scholarly critics to deflect attention from the specifically colonial dimensions of their psychological and political
themes.

I do not mean to suggest that students of Conrad and Kipling
have uniformly overlooked the colonial themes in their works. Ir-
ving Howe, Norman Sherry, and Avrom Fleishman, to name just a
few of Conrad's interpreters, have written at length about these
themes; Fleishman, in particular, has focused attention on the colonial coordinates of Conrad's political vision. A number of books

also address the colonial theme in general, notably Alan Sandison's *The Wheel of Empire*, Jonah Raskin's *The Mythology of Imperialism*, and Jeffry Meyer's *Fiction and the Colonial Experience*. None of these works, however, has taken for its point of departure the interest in the colonialist himself—his genesis, aspirations, achievements, and frustrations—that seems to have inspired Conrad and Kipling and certainly inspired many of their early readers.

My own interest in such questions grows out of my experience as a Peace Corps volunteer in the highlands of Kenya, where the colonial world survives in the shape of the land, the look of certain buildings, the way people dress and speak and think and earn their livings. I wanted to get to know the ghosts who hovered around the abandoned pit head at Macalder's Mine in South Nyanza and who shared the rooms of handsome ruined farmhouses with African squatters, Peace Corps volunteers, chickens, and snakes. And I wanted more than an anecdotal or abstract introduction. So I turned first to Conrad and then, with increasing respect, to Kipling. (Afterwards I read E. M. Forster, Graham Greene, and Joyce Cary, but their insights strike me as elaborations, for the most part, of the great pioneering portraits produced by Kipling and Conrad.)

What I acquired was a new awareness of the rich intricacy of Kipling's and Conrad's fiction and of the social and psychological insights to be found there. These insights into the special and extinct life world of the colonialist are, to my mind at least, intrinsically interesting. But they also cast light on the civilization from which the colonialist emerged. "All Europe contributed to the making of Kurtz," observes Marlow in *Heart of Darkness*,[5] and both Conrad and Kipling insist that we accept the colonialist as "one of us."

Kipling's soldiers and imperial officers are different men, in different situations, and under different pressures than Conrad's commercial adventurers. And Kipling brings to their delineation a set of values profoundly at odds with Conrad's. In spite of these differences, however, there are significant and illuminating similarities between the two sets of portraits. Both challenge the romantic image of colonial life; both insist on the claustrophobic isolation of the small European stations lost in the immensity of Asia or Africa, the persistent strangeness of the local peoples, the endurance of banality and meanness in the most exotic settings, and the bitter irony of privileges purchased at the price of exile from home and homeland.

And both elucidate—sometimes inadvertently—the painful contradictions of the colonialist's situation. They suggest, for instance, that the very experiences that impel Europeans to seek power and wealth in the colonial world ultimately disable them in important ways for the practical achievement of their goals. In Conrad's fiction, the desperate audacity and arrogance that helps men like Jim and Kurtz to take power also blinds them to fatal flaws in their perceptions of themselves and others. Drawn to the colonial world in hopes of finding refuge from certain humiliating definitions imposed on them in Europe, they struggle unsuccessfully to transform the communities they invade into living negations of these definitions, affirmations of their own egotistical illusions. In Kipling's fiction the experiences of harsh discipline, abandonment, and humiliation that are an accepted part of the future imperialist's education instill both strong impulses to dominate and a terror of isolation and exposure that makes effective exercise of authority impossible. The Indian stories are full of colonial figures who perceive themselves as existing at the very limits of exposure and anxiety, and who therefore refuse to venture out of their clubs and compounds into the Indian community. By creating such figures, and by treating them as representative, Kipling and Conrad suggest that in choosing a colonial career Europeans condemn themselves to attempting a role they are ill equipped to play. Their works challenge the image of the colonialist—as a manly, fair, and supremely self-confident ruler of lesser men—that was emerging in popular adventure tales and jingoistic journalism at the time they wrote.

Their fiction testifies as well against the promise of autonomy and authority that they see as the chief attraction of the colonial world. Their most adventurous colonialists find life under the domination of public and private powers at home intolerable, and flee to the colonies in order to recover some measure of independence. But in doing so, Conrad and Kipling show, these men make themselves

As in Wells

the agents of the very powers they flee—of government power, in the case of Kipling's Indian imperialists, and of private interests, in the case of Conradian figures such as Lingard, Kurtz, and Gould. Financed and equipped by these interests, they pursue their own private projects of escape and empire-building. But even if they succeed in setting themselves up as lords beyond the limits of European control, the moment of independence is fleeting, even illusory. For they are themselves the outriders of the very forces they hope to elude—and their paid agents. Whatever control they establish must pass inevitably from their own hands to the hands of those who sponsored them, and they must suffer once again the constrictions and humiliations they hoped to escape. The fate of Kipling's colonial officers and of Conrad's freebooting traders is on one level the same: to discover, each in a different way and at the moment of apparent liberation, the fact of their own continued subjugation.

Thus Conrad's portraits of the colonialist, and Kipling's as well, resolve themselves into images of inadequacy and frustration. Conrad's argument is against the whole venture, and his rhetorical strategy seems to be to show that even the best Europeans are not clear-sighted and unselfish enough to preside over communities so different from their own as those they encounter in the colonial world. Kipling, on the other hand, is a strong defender of the idea of colonial domination, and his purpose in publicizing its contradictions and the inadequacies of its agents is to make a case for revising the system. Indeed, the entire imaginative and rhetorical thrust of his later Indian works is toward the persuasive delineation of a new program of selection and education for future imperial rulers, a program that would do away with the psychologically crippling experiences generated under the existing system.

In concentrating on these social and psychological themes I have tended to ignore other, equally important, aspects of Kipling's and Conrad's works, particularly their aesthetic dimensions. The omission does not imply a feeling on my part that there are no connections to be made between form and content, social vision and its aesthetic expression. On the contrary, these connections remain one of the most interesting subjects of study for students of Kipling and

Conrad. Kipling, for instance, seems to have modeled his early style
on the modes of discourse characteristic of the imperial service elite.
"He told his tale in few words, as it might have been an official
report," observes the narrator in "William the Conqueror," speaking of that story's hero, a young officer in the Irrigation Service.[6]
And we see the narrator himself striving to approximate this ideal
in his own manner of delivery, pressing for a certain spareness of
presentation. At another point in the same story, a newspaper
editor, asking the hero for a report from the famine zone to which
he is being sent, advises him to write "nothing sensational . . . but
just plain facts about who is doing what."[7] The beauty of this advice, in Kipling's case, is that his material is so intrinsically sensational, so exotic and full of incident, that he does not need to choose
between sensationalism and a more professional posture of self-
constrained attention to the facts. When Kipling's narrators stum-
ble, it is not in exaggerating the horror of the events they recount,
but in appearing to be so at home with horror that we recognize
the artificiality of their nonchalance, see them for a moment as excited and insecure young men straining to enact a particular conception of manliness, and losing in the process the capacity for honest
response that we identify with authentic maturity. But perhaps the
men Kipling admired were themselves incapable of such a response.
They may have been, of necessity, what Kipling called "armoured"
men,[8] men who found it necessary to curtail reflection and feeling
in order to protect themselves against wounding insights and dis-
abling emotions.

By creating a narrative voice out of the discourse of these men—
their telegrams and directives and memos, their official reports and
unofficial shop talk—Kipling adds an extra dimension to his portrait of British India and a new voice to the world of serious fiction.
But he may also trap himself within the limited and unreflective
perspective enforced by this world. Like any armored man, he is
constricted in his movements by the unyielding forms within which
he must live. Thus the particular kind of armored discourse he feels
compelled to adopt may cut him off from a kind of exploration that
Conrad sees as the very source of artistic insight.

"The artist descends within himself . . . ," Conrad writes in the Preface to The Nigger of the "Narcissus," to that part of our nature which, because of the warlike conditions of existence, is necessarily kept out of sight within the more resisting and hard qualities—like the vulnerable body within a steel armour."[9] Certain possibilities of elaboration are available only to those who will struggle, as Conrad does, in his fiction, to think and speak across the full range of human experience, to acknowledge and explore complexities beyond the range of view and verbal possibility of a style developed in emulation of instrumental prose and club-room anecdote. Kipling's reduction of his own range of vision and voice, a reduction that almost certainly played a significant role in winning him precocious fame, may well have contributed in the long run to the failure to develop that so disappointed his early admirers.

Conrad's style is in many ways the antithesis of Kipling's. While Kipling favors, in the Indian stories at least, a spare and aggressively confident style, Conrad tends to develop and juxtapose narrative voices in a manner that registers the all but overwhelming difficulty of understanding, interpreting, and expressing experience. In his work, too, the style and the colonial subject matter are organically connected. Conrad's narrators speak as they do in part because their explorations have taken them beyond the borders of conventional experience and have revealed the poverty of conventional wisdom. Sailing up the Congo, witnessing the atrocities committed by European invaders and the enigmatic responses of their victims, Marlow falls into a profound confusion. "You lost your way on that river," he remarks, "as you would in a desert, and butted all day long against shoals, trying to find the channel, till you thought yourself bewitched and cut off for ever from everything you had known once."[10] In his narration, as in his navigation, Marlow manifests the explorer's most essential virtue, determination. But because his discoveries are so at odds with all he has known, because he can find no coherent and consoling way to explain what he has seen, because, finally, he can find no social agency capable of combatting the evil that is being done, his report is neither clear, nor "well-organized," nor confident in its assertions. Time and again he advances a proposition, pauses as if he has run up against some hidden shoal, and then backs off, qualifying or contradicting himself or approaching his subject from a different point of view. In this and other ways, his narrative style, the style of the best colonial novels, reflects the impact on thought and speech of the incidents narrated.

If I ignore the aesthetic dimension of the works I study, then, it is neither because I do not appreciate this dimension nor because I see it as separate in any ultimate way from the dimensions I do discuss. On the contrary, I hope that the insights developed here may prepare the ground for a study of Conrad's and Kipling's style that will disclose significant parallels between narrated action and the action of narration in their works, and will deepen our understanding of the aesthetic dimension itself.

Kipling and Conrad both had first-hand experience of the conditions of life they identify as shaping the colonialist's character and consciousness. In the chapters that follow I will be discussing not only the colonial dimension of their works but also their own experiences of colonialism and the role these experiences played in shaping their portraits of colonial life.

1

KIPLING'S EMPIRE

And the measure of our torment is the measure of our youth.
God help us, for we knew the worst too young!
KIPLING, "Gentlemen-Rankers"

Rudyard Kipling, born in Bombay in 1865, spent his early childhood and young manhood among the service elite of the Indian Empire, a group composed largely of civilian and military officers of the Raj. Raymond Williams, describing this group's place in the British ruling class, writes: "Only part of the [ruling] class was quite wholly in command: able to live on its property and investments, or to move directly into the central metropolitan institutions. A much larger part had a harder and humbler function. The education of these people, essentially, was as servants of a system to which they belonged only as functionaries. And it was they who went out to the edges of the system, facing its realities directly."[1] A series of traumatic abandonments—early exile from home, bitter impotence during the first years at public school, and exile again, this time to the outposts of Empire—prepared the members of this group for imperial service. These concrete experiences reinforced many of the lessons of schoolroom and chapel. They taught not open-mindedness and generosity, but authoritarian rigidity, respect for power, and love of domination. These qualities were considered useful in men who were to become, in George Orwell's words, "the shock absorbers of the bourgeoisie."[2]

In recalling his youth, Kipling once spoke of "a certain darkness into which the soul of the young man sometimes descends—a horror of desolation, abandonment, and realised worthlessness, which is one of the most real of the hells in which we are compelled to walk."[3] In thus describing his own situation, Kipling presents a vivid impression of the psychological state identified by T. W. Adorno and Erich Fromm with authoritarian patterns of behavior. Adorno and Fromm agree that the authoritarian, whether leader or willing follower of a despotic movement, makes his political decisions from an often unconscious foundation of extreme insecurity. They agree, futhermore, that the primary experience predisposing one to authoritarianism is that of terrifying isolation and impotence in a hostile world.[4]

Kipling was first exposed to this kind of isolation as a child of five when, in accordance with Anglo-Indian custom, he and his sister were sent "home" to England so that they might not be contaminated spiritually or physically by India. Since Kipling's parents did not want to impose on their relatives in England, they chose guardians for their children from newspaper advertisements. They accompanied the children to England, saw them settled at their new Southsea foster home, and then left without explanation, farewell, or promise of return.

This mode of departure intensified the children's feelings of abandonment and worthlessness. Years later, Kipling's sister wrote: "Looking back . . . I think the real tragedy of our early days, apart from Aunty's bad temper and unkindness to my brother, sprang from our inability to understand why our parents had deserted us. We had no preparation or explanation; it was like a double death, or rather, like an avalanche that had swept away everything happy and familiar . . . We felt that we had been deserted, 'almost as much as on a doorstep,' and what was the reason?"[5] Interpreting their abandonment as a punishment, the two sought diligently for a crime. Kipling may have come to see his offense in what would now be called oedipal terms. "Gow's Watch," one of the many works in which he seems to be exploring and rewriting his own childhood, tells the story of a young prince's incestuous affair with his stepmother.[6] The affair occurs, Kipling suggests, because the prince has been kept at home too long, instead of being sent off on adventures. If the five-year-old Kipling did interpret his exile as punishment for oedipal crimes, this might help explain his otherwise puzzling silence concerning the treatment he received at Southsea. While he was there he never complained either to his family or to his relatives, although he was cruelly tormented by the "Aunty" who was his surrogate mother.

In his autobiography, *Something of Myself* (1937), Kipling describes his six years at Southsea as a time of "calculated torture" in a "House of Desolation." His guardian, a fanatically religious widow, set out to break the spirit of her precocious ward. Rudyard's few pleasures were noted and used to punish him: he enjoyed reading, so his books were taken away; he needed his sister's support, so she was taught to distrust him and they were often kept apart. He was isolated and humiliated in numerous ways. Visitors and new acquaintances were warned that he was a "moral leper," and for having concealed a bad school report, he was made to walk through town to school with a sign "Liar" on his back. The widow and her son beat him regularly.[7]

In an effort to elude his tormentors, the young boy sought refuge in the realms of art and fantasy. During long hours of solitary confinement in the cellar, the future poet of Empire would play at being Robinson Crusoe, the archetypal imperialist: "My apparatus was a coconut shell strung on a red cord, a tin trunk, and a piece of packing-case which kept off any other world. Thus fenced about, everything inside the fence was quite real . . . If the bit of board fell, I had to begin the magic all over again . . . The magic, you see, lies in the ring or fence that you take refuge in."[8] Kipling's basement trading post is an early version of the circumscribed realities within which he later sought refuge from dangers real and imagined. To follow were the little worlds of the club, the mess hall, the engine room, and the larger circle of the Empire. Each had its own language and arcane knowledge, which Kipling delighted in mastering and which, like the child's fence, excluded outsiders while bestowing a reassuring "reality" on everything within its bounds.

At Southsea Kipling's defenses proved inadequate. Toward the end of his term there he suffered hallucinations and nervous collapse. He was also found to be almost blind. For Kipling, then, the "certain darkness" of desolation and abandonment fell first of all during his more than six years in Southsea. The impact of the experience can hardly be exaggerated, for as Kipling himself observes, it is the case with children that "what comes to them they accept as eternally established."[9]

Kipling recognizes that a basic transformation in his personality occurred at Southsea, and in the short story "Baa Baa, Black Sheep" (1888) he achieves a bitter triumph of self-analysis. The story's hero, Punch, closely resembles Kipling himself; the theme is the destruction of Punch's self-confidence and trust and the emergence of hatred, fear, and suspicion as the dominant elements of his personality.

Punch's life begins in India, where he is given all the support he needs to deal confidently and creatively with his gradually expanding world. Then comes the sudden exile to England. When Punch first meets the family who are to be his guardians, he approaches them "without fear, as he had been accustomed to do."[10] But the old generous customs no longer hold. Abandoned by his family, tormented beyond endurance by his guardians, Punch finds himself ignorant and isolated in a hostile world: "When a matured man discovers that he has been deserted by Providence, deprived of his God, and cast, without help, comfort, or sympathy, upon a world which is new and strange to him, his despair . . . is generally supposed to be impressive. A child, under exactly similar circumstances as far as its knowledge goes, cannot very well curse God and die" (p. 333).

Instead, he must attempt to adjust to the new realities of his condition, and this is what Punch sets out to do. He develops a new "gospel of life": "Aunty Rosa . . . had the power to beat him with many stripes. It was unjust and cruel, and Mamma and Papa would never have allowed it. Unless perhaps, as Aunty Rosa seemed to imply, they had sent secret orders. In which case he was abandoned indeed. It would be discreet in the future to propitiate Aunty Rosa" (p. 343).

In somewhat the same spirit, Punch goes to great lengths of self-abasement to maintain his sister's affection:

> "You're my own brother, though you are—though Aunty Rosa says you're Bad, and Harry says you're a little coward. He says that if I pulled your hair hard, you'd cry."
> "Pull, then," said Punch.
> Judy pulled gingerly.
> "Pull harder—as hard as you can! There! I don't mind how much you pull it *now*. If you'll speak to me same as ever I'll let you pull it as much as you like—pull it out if you like." (p. 347)

The boy whose reaction to his first beating at Aunty Rosa's hands is "But—I'm—I'm not an animal!" (p. 343) will now endure the torments of a younger sister in order to win approval and protection. And he is ready to treat other, weaker beings with brutality. So complete is the transformation that when after six years his mother returns, Punch's first thoughts are: "She's too little to hurt any one . . . and if I said I'd kill her, she'd be afraid" (p. 365). Although the children return to their family at the end of the story, Kipling refuses the easy resolution of a conventional happy ending:

> "There! 'Told you so," says Punch. "It's all different now, and we are just as much Mother's as if she had never gone."
> Not altogether, O Punch, for when young lips have drunk deep of the bitter waters of Hate, Suspicion, and Despair, all the Love in the world will not wholly take away that knowledge; though it may turn darkened eyes for a while to the light, and teach Faith where no Faith was. (p. 368)

Punch's world view and view of himself have been altered irreversibly by his descent into impotence and isolation. He will be disposed in the future to fight any outsider, defer to any powerful authority, mistrust any claim to kinship. And any talk of progress and humanity will find only a mocking echo in the darkness of his heart.

The truth of Kipling's final judgment in "Baa Baa, Black Sheep" is borne out by the very tone of the story. False light alternates with convincing darkness throughout. At the beginning and end, when the children are with their family, the language is that of the conventional sentimental childhood tale. In the early pages Punch "*thmacks*" Judy, or entertains her by the seashore with an "ickle trab" he has found. But as the horror of existence at Aunty Rosa's closes in, the sentimental language disappears and the story becomes a simple and frequently eloquent record of a child's life in hell. The puppets become real people. Only at the end, when the children are back with their mother, does Kipling fall once again into the sentimentalized version of childhood. Thus the tone of the story bears out the narrator's dark prophecy. That narrator, Punch grown to manhood, cannot persuasively describe the light he cannot see.

Given the compound horrors of Kipling's life at Southsea, and the bitter eloquence of his testimony, it is natural to conclude that the torments he endured were due to some terrible eccentricity of fate. Yet Kipling's early exile and harsh subjugation were the common lot of many Anglo-Indian children. Any British family who could afford the expense sent their youngsters to England. The luckier ones went to live with kindly relatives, but many found themselves the wards of unsympathetic strangers. One contemporary observer wrote of children "for whose education and comfort large fees have been paid, being half starved, badly taught, and made little better than domestic drudges by those who ought honestly to have treated them well: and all this time the children were compelled to write to their parents elaborately false statements speaking of the kindness they received, and of the comforts they enjoyed."[11] Kipling's Southsea experience and the deep psychological scars it left may have been rather the rule than the exception among his fellows.

Following his years at Southsea, Kipling was sent off to school. The change was a mixed blessing, for he found himself once again alone and confronted with powerful enemies. The public schools of England provided each new student with a formal introduction to the condition of "desolation, abandonment, and realized worthlessness" that Kipling wrote of experiencing in his

youth. The United Services College, Kipling's school, was particularly rough, for it took in many students who had proved
troublesome elsewhere, and it lacked the civilizing traditions of
some older schools. In *Something of Myself* Kipling passes cryptically
over his early experiences there, saying only that his first term was
"horrible" and his first year and a half "not pleasant."[12] *Stalky and
Co.* (1899), his collection of stories on schoolboy life, briefly describes the bullying of younger students, but focuses primarily on
the experiences of three older boys. When there is torturing to be
done, they do it.

More explicit evidence of the torments of the young students
comes from L. C. Dunsterville, Kipling's schoolboy friend and the
original "Stalky." In his memoirs, Dunsterville describes several of
the methods popular at U.S.C. One of these, called "hanging," involved lowering a student down a five-story stairwell: "The condemned criminal was taken to the top floor . . . His eyes were then
blindfolded, and a rope with a slip-knot placed under his arms. A
certain amount of slack was allowed for the first drop to give an uncomfortable jerk."[13] Then the victim was lowered until an assistant
executioner on the ground floor gave the signal for the final drop.
In one case Dunsterville recalls, the signal was premature, and the
blindfolded victim broke his leg. This torture, and many others as
well, are unconscious reenactments of the schoolboy's common
fate: to be hurled blind and powerless into an alien world where
some kind of fall is inevitable. The lessons taught were clear: submit, endure, and seek revenge on the next contingent of novices.

Thus the lessons of Southsea were reinforced at school. Not just
Kipling, but every schoolboy was the subject of torments and humiliations. If he were willing, he might become the servant of an
older student, thus trading his freedom for minimal security, and
balancing his humiliation against whatever status his master's position might confer on him. If he sought to maintain his dignity and
autonomy, he was in for torments such as those chronicled in *Tom
Brown's Schooldays*. And not every headmaster was an Arnold, nor
every new boy as strong as Tom. Even at its best, then, this method
of education encouraged adjustment and conformity, rather than

principled independence and cooperation. Safety lay either in propi-
tiating one's tormentors by acts of submission or in impressing
them by precocious emulation. In both cases the young boy's self-
confidence was crippled—in the first by humiliation, in the second
by his implicit dependence on external criteria of approval. And the
habit of displacing hostility onto weaker parties while submitting
without question to the stronger became ever more deeply in-
grained.

A major function of public school education was the preparation
of future imperial servants. The harsh discipline and rugged life of
school was intended to fit students for a vocation in the lonely outposts of Empire. For the greatest abandonment was the last: the
young man's exile to a hostile and alien land. Kipling's parents were
unable to afford a university education for their son, and his poor
eyesight precluded a military career, so they found him a job as an
apprentice newspaperman in Lahore, where they lived. Ironically,
the attraction of India was no longer what it had been during the
years at Southsea. Kipling had grown interested in the intellectual
and artistic life of England, and had gained through his uncle Edward Burne-Jones a certain familiarity with artistic society. He had
also fallen in love. So once again a journey "home" meant the sacrifice of hopes and love, exile from a secure and benevolent world.

What is more, Kipling was returning not to the idyllic life of his
early childhood, but to the duties and manifold discomforts of life as
a journalist in India. Luckier than most of his contemporaries in
having his family so near, he shared his peers' struggle to survive
and succeed in spite of the harsh climate and constant illnesses: "I
never worked less than ten hours and seldom more than fifteen per
diem," he later wrote. "I had fever too, regular and persistent, to
which I added for a while chronic dysentery. Yet I discovered that a
man can work with a temperature of 104, even though next day he
has to ask the office who wrote the article . . . my world was filled
with boys, but a few years older than I, who lived utterly alone,
and died from typhoid mostly at the regulation age of
twenty-two."[14] The strain took its toll. During the almost seven
years he spent in India (1882–1889) Kipling suffered two more break-

downs, bouts of "staleness and depression," which he attributed to "overwork, plus fever and dysentery."[15] No wonder that, echoing his name for the house at Southsea, he once described India as a "house of torment."[16] And perhaps his frequent references to Queen Victoria as "the Widow" stem in part from this same identification, with the Empress of India replacing the widow at Southsea.[17] The realm of darkness had not diminished, but enlarged.

For most of those who went out to the Empire, the crisis of abandonment was compounded, rather than mitigated, by official policy; Michael Edwardes, in *Bound for Exile*, writes that "the principle of pushing its employees in at the deep end in the hope that they would soon learn to swim remained an integral part of Indian Civil Service policy. A young man was sent straight off into the district, given a few weeks to appreciate the difficulties, and then expected to deal with some of them. He would have to try cases which were apparently simple, but, in fact enmeshed in contradictions and dubious evidence." Thus the young British officer in India found himself, in Edwardes's words, "alone, ignorant, and responsible."[18] Judging people whose language and customs he knew only slightly, aware of the fact that they would exploit his ignorance even as they deferred to his authority, he must have felt once again abandoned, threatened, and worthless, must have raged once again at his blindness and impotence, and must have wondered whether the twin ropes of his sanity and authority would hold. As at school, the surest defense lay in rigid conformity, submission to one's superiors, and a compensatory assertion of strength against the weak, in this case the Indians.

Thus, by a series of abandonments, the imperial civil servant's character was molded. Each experience of isolation and impotence confirmed a view of the world as implacably hostile, a view of the individual as utterly insignificant. Moreover, each experience prepared the victim to assume an authoritarian stance: to obey orders, grapple himself to a powerful group, channel his aggression outward against weaker parties. With the reiteration of these crises, many young men must have come to see dominance and submission as the only categories of human relations, and to interpret all ap-

peals to traditional ethics and ideas of equality as attempts at deception. There is evidence of acquiescence in such a world view both in
Kipling's art and in the history of the imperial service elite.

In his fiction, Kipling presents a number of heroes — the
common soldier, the freebooter, and the imperial officer. He
celebrates the virtues and indicates the weaknesses of each, always
from an authoritarian perspective. But the group to which he is
most committed, whose values and aspirations he most fully shares,
is that of the imperial service elite, the field officers — civil and
military — of the Raj.

The Kipling hero lowest on the social and psychological ladder of
power is the common British soldier. Kipling portrays the soldier as
an essential component in the machinery of domination and as a
figure motivated by the urge to destroy. "Speaking roughly," he
writes in "The Drums of the Fore and Aft" (1888), "you must
employ either blackguards or gentlemen, or, best of all, blackguards
commanded by gentlemen, to do butcher's work with efficiency
and despatch."[19] Kipling sees the soldier's work as necessary, then.
But he also finds it appealing, for soldiers act out the common authoritarian dream of total destructiveness, in which the dark under-
currents of hostility fed by years of impotent rage are allowed to
surface, control the personality, and express themselves in acts of
untempered aggression.

Because Kipling himself dreams of the perverse catharsis his soldier heroes actually achieve, he presents them realistically and sympathetically: "Mulvaney, Ortheris and Learoyd are Privates in B
Company of a Line Regiment, and personal friends of mine. Collec-
tively I think . . . they are the worst men in the regiment as far as
genial blackguardism goes."[20] The three characters' geniality resides
solely in such qualities as kindliness to harmless children, obedience
to powerful superiors, and a penchant for rather comic acts of deception and manipulation. For the rest, they are men whose greatest pleasure in life is killing, and whose pastimes are brawling,
drinking, thieving, and looting. Yet Kipling so successfully com-

municates his enjoyment of the three that it is difficult to describe them for what they are without losing completely the tone of many of the stories in which they appear.

Several stories collected in *Soldiers Three* provide real insights into the life of the common soldier of the day. "With the Main Guard" (1888), for instance, conveys a vivid sense both of bloody battle and of the dreadful monotony of garrison life in India. "On Greenhow Hill" (1890) shows how deeply Kipling understood the process by which the urge to destroy was instilled in the common soldier. The three privates are waiting in ambush for an Indian deserter who has been sniping at them for several nights. As they wait, Learoyd recalls his adolescent love for an English girl, and wonders for a moment if the deserter hasn't left his regiment because of a woman. Mulvaney checks him for "suggestin' invidious excuses for the man Stanley's goin' to kill," but encourages him to tell his story.[21] Learoyd proceeds; the burden of his tale is that for a time in England his sense of love and community drew him toward positive feelings and actions, but that the fatal illness of his fiancée and the hostile indifference of English society destroyed his hope. His narrative clearly indicates that the thwarting of love on a human and social level induces a love of destruction, and this vital insight is reinforced throughout the story. In the final paragraphs, for instance, Learoyd's bitter bereavement at the death of his beloved is juxtaposed with Ortheris's deeply sensual murder of the deserter.

Kipling is clearly aware that libidinal forces can become destructive. Throughout the story he describes Ortheris's commitment to killing in phallic terms: "He jerked the cartridge out of the breech-block into the palm of his hand. ' 'Ere's my chaplin,' he said, and made the venomous black-headed bullet bow like a marionette. ' 'E's goin' to teach a man all about which is which, an' wot's true, after all, before sundown'" (p. 217). The particular ferocity of Ortheris's hatred is due, the story suggests, to the fact that he has enjoyed even less nurturing than his companions: "He had not been nursed by many women in his life" (p. 212). With no experience of love to give him a sense of his own and other people's worth, and with a deep fund of bitterness at having been so deprived, Ortheris uses a rifle to establish a place for himself in the community. A mere cipher, unwanted, inessential, and powerless, he proves by killing that he does exist, that his existence makes a difference to others, and that his power is in some ways at least absolute. He establishes, too, a terrible negative community, based on acts of murder rather than on support. Kipling dramatizes, with brilliant lucidity, Erich Fromm's insight into the source of authoritarian destructiveness: "The more the drive toward life is thwarted, the stronger is the drive toward the destruction . . . *Destructiveness is the outcome of unlived life.*"[22]

Kipling's insights into the dynamics of this process and his sympathy for its victims are impressive, but he shows sympathy as well for their twisted values and deeds. The last words of "On Greenhow Hill," with their identification of the artist and the sniper, of creation and destruction, suggest the degree to which Kipling shares the traits of his characters: "He was staring across the valley [at the dead man], with the smile of the artist who looks on the completed work" (p. 231). In fact, dreams of destruction are the implicit source of many of Kipling's fictional creations; they are also the legacy of his own abandonment to a hostile world.

Kipling licenses his soldiers not only to kill but also to torture and rob their victims. In the poem "Loot" (1890), for instance, the speaker gives a few lessons in these arts:

> Now remember when you're 'acking round a gilded
>   Burma god
> That 'is eyes is very often precious stones;
> An' if you treat a nigger to a dose o' cleanin'-rod
> 'E's like to show you everything 'e owns.[23]

These lines have been excused as mere exercises in dramatic monologue, but I doubt that Kipling wrote them as such. For one thing, this poem belongs to a group that Kipling wrote not just about soldiers but for them, and many in the group are explicitly didactic. What is more, in *Stalky and Co.* (1899) Kipling supports looting quite explicitly. The reader is invited to "Just imagine Stalky let loose on the south side of Europe with a sufficiency of Sikhs and a reasonable prospect of loot. Consider it quietly."[24] The last sentence, with its invitation to savour thoughts of mass destruction, is the most telling. Kipling sees looting as a minor prerogative of the soldier, a complement and inducement to his central vocation of destruction.

The only limitation that Kipling places on his soldiers' licensed excesses is that they take place within a larger context of absolute loyalty to military authority. Mulvaney, the most accomplished rogue of the group, is also the most untiring defender of his officers' superiority. He never sides with the men against their commanders, and is always willing, as in "The Big Drunk Draf'" (1888), to suggest extra-legal methods of keeping unruly troops in line. Like the three schoolboy heroes of *Stalky and Co.*, the grown-up children of *Soldiers Three* only appear to be rebels. In fact they are dedicated defenders of their masters' authority. As licensed outlaws, they boast of their defiance and take privileges denied to their more authentically rebellious comrades, while still enjoying the security of their larger submission. In the end, however, Kipling demonstrates that the privileges granted to the common soldier, no matter how crafty he may be in exploiting them, by no means make up for his exclusion from the larger possibilities of life. Even in authoritarian terms, destructiveness is an unsatisfying way of dealing with a sense of isolation and sterility. Unlike domination, it leaves the individual alone, without living servants or accumulated wealth to attest to his superiority.

Kipling's second imperial hero, the freebooting gentleman-rover, does without official license and support, and so can take even more liberties with conventional codes of conduct than the soldier. A member of a "wholly unauthorized horde," he disdains the dependency of his brothers in government and the military. The freebooters of "The Lost Legion" (1893) boast:

> Our fathers they left us their blessing—
>   They taught us, and groomed us, and crammed;
> But we've shaken the Clubs and the Messes
>   To go and find out and be damned.[25]

Having "shaken" the fear of exposure which binds his fellow imperialists to the club and the mess, the freebooter can pursue his

goals of domination and wealth without any of the restraints imposed by social custom or the unsympathetic restrictions of a central
government.

Nor is he deterred by any internalized ethical standards. Nick
Tarvin, the American hero of *The Naulahka* (1891), having come to
India in search of loot, pursues his goal without compunction. He
observes of his fiancée that "she could not know, and probably
could not have imagined, how little his own sense of the square
thing had to do with any system of morality."[26] Kipling clearly admires Tarvin's utter lack of scruples and the spurious freedom it
confers. He portrays him as one of "the irrepressible race who stride
booted into the council-halls of kings, and demand concessions for
oil-boring from Arracan to the Peshin" (p. 201). Beside such men,
the more tradition-bound Anglo-Indians pale. Kipling describes the
British Tarvin meets as talking "as gypsies might talk by the roadside a little before the horses are put into the caravan . . . they
hoped one day to be able to rest . . . One of them even envied Tarvin for coming to the state with his fresh eye and his lively belief in
the possibility of getting something out of the land beside a harvest
of regrets" (p. 234). Both parties' goals are exploitation, but the
freebooter's drives are less repressed by custom and law.

Kipling's freebooters, like his other imperial heroes, are firmly
rooted in historical reality. In Kipling's time, personal kingdoms
were still being carved out of Africa and the Far East by men like
the second Rajah Brooke of Sarawak and Cecil Rhodes of South
Africa. Company agents, often with their own private armies, were
penetrating ever deeper into unexplored and unexploited regions.
And gradually the direct rule of the British was beginning to appear
unnecessarily cumbersome in the light of less formal types of largely
economic domination. *The Naulahka* anticipates the transfer of
power from the Empire-weary British government to eager European and American neocolonialists. But it is perhaps a distortion on
Kipling's part to describe his freebooters as wholly unauthorized
and totally independent. In many cases they worked not as mere individuals, but as the representatives of capital, the lieutenants of
industry.

Tarvin's schemes illuminate the hypocrisy of many "aid" programs. In order to conceal his true purpose — the theft of the jewels that are the accumulated wealth of the state — he deceives the maharajah into investing large sums of money in a hopeless plan to dam a river. "The futile damming of the barren Amet" serves his stated purpose, which is quite simply "to raise a dust to hide one's ends" (pp. 199–200). Kipling approves this type of deception as completely as he does that practiced by his other imperial heroes, and although Tarvin's schemes come to nothing, he is allowed the consolation of blowing up the dam.

Unlicensed but also unbound, the freebooter would seem to be the ideal authoritarian hero; yet Kipling depicts him only occasionally. Perhaps the very autonomy of the freebooter made it hard for Kipling, so concerned with domination in a social sense, so dependent on external reinforcement for his own security, to identify with him. Inclusion in a large and powerful community is important to Kipling; although he denies the freebooter his place in the official community, he gives him a community of his own, portraying him as part of a "wholly unauthorized horde," a "Lost Legion."

Unlike soldiers and freebooters, the members of the imperial service elite are both licensed and relatively unrepressed. Kipling was bound by birth and education to this caste; only his vocation as journalist kept him at its periphery, for its members were mainly district officers, military men, engineers, or field officers in some other branch of the government. Kipling sometimes describes these men in terms of Victorian ideals of service and self-sacrifice, but his more convincing stories illuminate them with a less flattering light. In these, the colonial official appears as a genial but unscrupulous despot gratifying at once his urge to dominate and the Indian's need for domination.

Kipling never questions the latter need. He accepts and reiterates the commonplace identification of the Indians with children who must remain under protective custody: "Never forget that unless the outward and visible signs of Our Authority are always before a native he is as incapable as a child of understanding what authority means, or where is the danger of disobeying it."[27] Kipling's own work could easily be introduced to challenge this assertion, for in several stories he portrays Indians who act with great restraint and assume important responsibilities. But such a challenge misses the point. Statements like the one above are not primarily generalizations based on experience, but ideological weapons in the imperialist's struggle for legitimation. Having labeled the Indian a child, the imperialist can argue that any rebellion stems not from rational political grievances, but from irrational impulses. He can argue, too, that his use of force to maintain control is necessary, since children are not rational creatures.

So labeled, the colonized are caught in a double bind. If they obey, they prove the contention that they need and want to be dominated. If they rebel, they prove only that domination is necessary. Moreover, some members of the colonized community, awed by the superior power of the imperialist forces, may actually come to believe that they are intrinsically inferior creatures. Trapped by being defined as children, demoralized by their sense of inferiority, they will be hard put to recover any self-confidence.

Nor does the imperialist desire any such recovery. His aim, as Kipling makes clear time and again, is to perpetuate the myth of intrinsic inferiority both in the colonies and at home. In fact, as Kipling argues in "The Man Who Would Be King" (1888), the imperialist's life depends on the maintenance of this illusion; the man who would be king must convince his subjects that he is not just accidentally and temporarily but fundamentally and permanently their superior.[28] Once he has enchained them with this illusion, they will no longer pose a constant threat. Drevoot, the vagabond king of Kafiristan in the story, uses his subjects' superstitions as well as modern rifles to establish his superiority. He is overthrown only when, forgetting the first rule of domination, he takes a wife from among his subjects and thus reveals his common mortality.

But to justify permanent imperial domination the metaphorical definition of the Indian as child must be qualified. Children grow up; their inferiority is only provisional. But the Indian, Kipling and his fellow imperialists claim, is a peculiar kind of child, one who will "never stand alone."[29] In "The Head of the District," Kipling's dying district officer is bidding farewell to his escort of native soldiers:

> "I do not know who takes my place. I speak now true talk, for I am as it were already dead, my children, — for though ye be strong men, ye are children."
>
> "And thou art our father and our mother," broke in Khoda Dad Khan with an oath. "What shall we do, now there is no one to speak for us, or to teach us to go wisely!"
>
> "There remains Tallantire Sahib. Go to him; he knows your talk and your heart. Keep the young men quiet, listen to the old men, and obey."[30]

Such conversations undoubtedly occurred; such bonds were formed. But Kipling's heroic district officer deliberately maintains his identity as father to the Indian's child. Even on his death bed, he utters not "true talk" but an enslaving lie. Or, more correctly, he utters a lie that has become, for his servants at least, an enslaving truth.

The district officer's interests, his desire to establish himself as an autocratic ruler, lead to his alliance with the most reactionary forces in Indian society. Kipling illuminates and endorses this alliance in "The Judgment of Dungara" (1888). The hero of the story, a young district officer, rules his territory with the help of the high priest of the local religion, Athon Dazé. Everything is running smoothly until two missionaries arrive on the scene; then both the Englishman and his pagan cohort feel threatened.

Why should the district officer see Christian missionaries as potential enemies? We are used to thinking of them as an imperial fifth column dividing once stable communities, obscuring the exploitative motives of European incursions, and providing pretexts for intervention. Missionaries have indeed served all these functions, but they have also provided colonized peoples with the knowledge and faith to begin overthrowing their masters. It is in this role that the missionaries of "The Judgment of Dungara" are cast. They serve a Christian "God of Things as They Should Be" who threatens not only Dazé's pagan "God of Things as They Are" but also the security of the district officer, who has a large psychological stake in maintaining the status quo. The district officer realizes this, and although he promises the missionaries "all the assistance in my power"[31] he actually abandons them to the mercies of the local priesthood.

The young Englishman's secret enjoyment of Dazé's offensive reveals the substratum of anarchy in his own apparently "civilized" personality. As is often the case, Kipling disguises the cruelty of his hero's acts by presenting them in comic form. When the well-dressed converts line up to welcome the British Collector to the thriving mission, they are suddenly overwhelmed by burning pains and break into a chaotic rabble. They interpret their agonies as the revenge of Dungara, their traditional god, but in fact the burning is caused by the juice of the plant fiber from which their clothes have been made, fiber provided by Athon Dazé. Dazé's plot succeeds, and the story ends with an image of triumphant disintegration: "the chapel and school have long since fallen back into jungle" (p. 59). Both Kipling and his hero approve the rout of knowledge and hope; watched over by the God of Things as They Are and the Empire, the Indians will remain in intellectual and political bondage.

What is it that the district officer gains from such a crippling of his subjects? What qualities make him heroic in Kipling's eyes? The description of the hero of "The Judgment of Dungara" provides the answer: he is "a knockkneed, shambling young man, naturally devoid of creed or reverence, with a longing for absolute power which his undesirable district gratified" (pp. 51-52). Unburdened by internal checks, licensed by his government as a despot, and able to operate without the immediate support of an external framework, the ideal district officer is able to gratify the need for absolute power that has been instilled in him during childhood. His escape from self-doubt and fear is the most satisfying one imaginable.

But the district officer of "The Judgment of Dungara" is only an ideal. Kipling recognized that most of his fellows in the imperial service had no such chance to achieve the gratifications of despotic autonomy, gratifications that, he thought, were their due. Instead they had to take what satisfaction they could from their role as servants of a powerful master. In "The Galley-Slave" (1890), he illuminates the situation of these men.

The poem, a dramatic monologue, unfolds as an extraordinary allegory of the psychological dynamics of the imperial servant. The speaker is a slave who has just been retired after years of service as an oarsman. The slave admits that his experience on the ship, which represents the British Raj, "broke" his "manhood," but he insists that he has gained a more heroic masculinity through his servitude: "If they wore us down like cattle, faith, we fought and loved like men." His reductive definition of manhood, however, only confirms his subjugation, for he has accepted his owners' limitations on what he can be. His description of life aboard the galley shows, furthermore, that he fights and loves not like a man but like an animal, with neither insight nor compassion. This conduct serves his masters' interests, too, for it makes him a willing oppressor of the other slaves in the galley, the "niggers" in the deepest hold who are threatening rebellion.

The slave takes his sense of masculinity from another source as well. Robbed of power himself, he identifies with the powerful ship. As a result, he comes to fear liberation, to serve willingly, and to respond to any threat to the institution by which he is enslaved as if it were a threat against himself. Bitter at his retirement, he takes pride in the badges of his servitude and curses his freedom:

> By the brand upon my shoulder, by the gall of clinging steel,
> By the welt the whips have left me, by the scars that never heal;
> By eyes grown old with staring through the sun-wash on the brine,
> I am paid in full for service—would that service still were mine![32]

It is difficult to imagine any of Kipling's fellow imperial servants actually making such a statement, but not hard at all, considering the educational program in which they were raised, to imagine them feeling this way. The poem offers a tragically perceptive picture of the process by which the sons of the English ruling class were reconciled to their roles as upper servants in the house of Empire.

Does Kipling actually wish to affirm the world the galley-slave presents — the submission, the reduction of potential, the displaced hostility, the masochistic pride in bondage? On one level, I believe, the answer is yes, for all of these are conditions with which he has cause to identify. Kipling is suggesting here, it seems to me, that although imperial servants are indeed slaves, their slavery is more satisfying than impotent isolation. But he is also acknowledging, if only implicitly, the disparity between the ideal self-image of the imperial service elite as a fellowship of lords and the reality of their status as privileged slaves.

This disparity seems to have been widely felt, for the local administrators of Kipling's time were engaged in a struggle both to hold off the imperial bureaucracy and to consolidate their status as heirs of a perpetual despotism.

In the Punjab, where Kipling lived and worked, British local administrators had been encouraged for years to act as virtual despots, guiding affairs in their districts on the basis of their own decisions. In the last decades of the century, however, this practice of direct rule was under attack on two fronts. The central bureaucracy, aided by improved communications and inspired by the theories of despotic utilitarianism, was tightening its control over officers in the field. At the same time, Indians educated in Western ideals of the government of law were calling for the end of arbitrary personal rule. The Congress party, through which this group coordinated its attack on the status quo, was founded in 1885. By 1900 it had spread throughout India and was widely regarded as the party of the new middle class of Indian professionals, government officials, and businessmen.[33]

The district officers of Kipling's time responded to these two threats by supporting the tradition of direct rule and by modifying it somewhat. The modifications were offered by a loosely organized group of British administrators called the Orientalists, who defended personal rule but argued in addition that this rule, to be effective, should be expressed in terms of Indian customs and traditions.[34] These were the only terms, the Orientalists argued, that the fundamentally benighted natives could understand. Since the Indians had proven themselves hopelessly incapable of appreciating Western values, they must be ruled in accordance with their own.

This argument was an extremely convenient one. It arose at exactly the time when Indians were proving themselves embarrassingly adept at using Western ideals to criticize British rule, and it provided an ideological rationale for the suppression both of these ideals and of the new class that was espousing them. As can be seen in Kipling's own stories, the Indian traditions to which the Orientalists appealed were the authoritarian ones of the old ruling class, the landowners and the priesthood. In "The Enlightenments of Pagett, M.P." (1890), the visiting dignitary is introduced by his host, a district officer, to an old Indian gentleman, and later asks the English official what the man thinks of the Congress movement: "Hates it all like poison . . . The worst of it is that he and his coreligionists, who are many, and the landed proprietors, also of Hindu race, are frightened and put out by this election business and by the importance we have bestowed on lawyers, pleaders, writers, and the like, who have, up to now, been in abject submission to them. They say little, but . . . all the glib bunkum in the world would not pay for their estrangement. They have controlled the land."[35] The Orientalist argument also served in the struggle against the central authorities, for the district officers, by virtue of his daily contact with the Indian community, could claim to be better informed as to its traditions than any bureaucrat. In the name of sympathetic rule, then, the Orientalists sought to realize the authoritarian ideal of absolute, autonomous power.

Kipling's vision in the imperial fiction of the eighties and nineties is that of the Orientalists. These were the men with whom he had grown up; he shared their fears, their values, and their aspirations. But he recognized their weaknesses as well. His stories and novels illuminate the source of these weaknesses, argue that they constitute a threat to imperial security, and offer a program for their eradication. Kipling's insights are frequently brilliant, his stories compelling. But his own authoritarian qualities, instilled during childhood, keep him from imagining morally palatable solutions to the problems he confronts.

2

UNBEARABLE BURDENS: KIPLING IN THE EIGHTIES

> *Take up the White Man's burden—*
> *Send forth the best ye breed—*
> *Go bind your sons to exile*
> *To serve your captives' need.*
>
> KIPLING, "The White Man's Burden"

Kipling's career as a professional writer began during his years as a journalist in India with publications in the English-language newspapers of the Raj. In some of the best stories of this period, Kipling suggests that early experiences often wound the British rulers of India in ways that prevent them from establishing the proper relationship—neither too intimate nor too distant—with their Indian subjects. Unable to endure the exposure and risk their work requires, some British officers fall into despair and madness, while others desert what should be their posts and retreat into the apparent security of the tiny British communities. Still others, unable to endure the banality of life in these artificial Englands, succumb to an even more fatal impulse and immerse themselves in the Indian community.

For Kipling, as an imperial artist, the problem of proper distance between European and Indian was aesthetic as well as political. To write about India, Kipling had to write about Indians. But how was he to learn about them and how present what he had learned? How close to them could he get without betraying his own community? Among the works of the eighties are certain stories in which he seems to be attempting a sympathetic identification with the Indian people and thereby to be developing a criticism of imperial rule. But this experiment is quickly abandoned, and Kipling adopts an artistic posture similar to the political stance his stories recommend.

The British position in India, Kipling suggests in his early stories, is becoming untenable. At the summer capital of Simla and in the clubs, the rulers distract themselves with petty intrigues, trivial quarrels, and endless gossip from the real issues of imperial rule. Within these enclaves existence is a matter of stale diversions and buried anxiety, while outside range the allied threats of disease, insurrection, and insanity. A few exceptional men face these threats and preserve the Raj, but more are desperately needed.

Why do so many imperial officers retreat from the physical and psychological exposure that their role on the front line requires of them? They do so, Kipling suggests, because they see themselves not as powerful rulers but as isolated and impotent exiles. This self-image, instilled in childhood and reinforced by the objective conditions of their life in India, drives them into the illusory refuge of the British compounds and clubs, from which they are unable to rule effectively.

"Baa Baa, Black Sheep" is Kipling's most eloquent testimony to the maiming effects of an Anglo-Indian childhood. Young Punch's confidence and inquisitiveness are destroyed by his guardians in England; first he retreats behind the flimsy walls of his books, then into the desperate posture of an animal at bay, turning on his tormentors with the threat of murder. Both responses foreshadow that of the frightened imperialist, all true self-assurance gone, who retreats into the club or turns with blind hostility against all Indians. Punch and the thousands like him intended for imperial service are prepared in advance to respond to India with fear and hostility.

The introduction to Empire that they are likely to receive only reinforces this predisposition. The four imperial servants in "At the End of the Passage" (1890) are described as "lonely folk who understood the dread meaning of loneliness. They were all under thirty years of age,—which is too soon for any man to possess that knowledge."[1] This judgment is borne out by events; the story records the suicide of one of them and the death of another through terror. The imperial policy of abrupt and total exposure to India makes a barely endurable situation even worse.

Furthermore, it robs the individual of the strength and confidence he will need as a ruler. Kipling makes this clear in "Gentlemen-Rankers" (1892), in which a well-born soldier fallen from his proper station explains his fall:

> We have done with Hope and Honour, we are lost to Love
> and Truth,
> We are dropping down the ladder rung by rung,
> And the measure of our torment is the measure of our
> youth.
> God help us, for we knew the worst too young![2]

Premature exposure, the soldier claims, has destroyed his confidence and hope. Significantly, he describes himself as a "black sheep," thus establishing his kinship in exile and despair with that other black sheep, the young Punch.

These stories and poems contain, then, an undertone of criticism directed against a system that treats its apprentices too harshly at first, then demands too much of them later. This theme is unexpected in Kipling, who most frequently speaks as an advocate of severe initiations, a critic of the "sheltered life system" of education.[3] Yet Kipling makes this criticism in the context of a broader position of support for authoritarian principles and in order to insure the continuance of imperial rule. He recognizes that if the initial abandonments are too severe, and subsequent assignments too difficult, the imperialist's urge to dominate may be overwhelmed by his sense of inadequacy and need for external support. Even if it is not, these forces may result in the imperialist's attempting to rule India from within the walls of the club, blindly and stupidly. The "gentlemen-rankers" of the poem are the most serious casualties:

trained to obey and to rule, they have been broken by the harshness of the training. Although they can still follow orders at times, they can no longer lead. Kipling insists that their failure and the larger failure of the system that produced them endanger the Empire. In major works like *Kim* and *The Jungle Book* he tries to imagine a system of education that will produce the instinct of domination without the corollary fears of isolation and deep conviction of inadequacy.

The role played by India in breaking the imperialist's spirit is documented by Kipling in several early stories. "The Strange Ride of Morrowbie Jukes" (1885) dramatizes the imperialist's nightmare vision of himself as an isolated and powerless victim of demonic Indian tormenters. Jukes, the story's protagonist, is an engineer working in the Indian desert. On a night when he is delirious with fever, he suddenly finds himself on horseback: "In one moment, for the brute bolted as straight as a die, the tent was left far behind, and we were flying over the smooth sandy soil at racing speed . . . The wretched beast went forward like a thing possessed, over what seemed to be a limitless expanse of moonlit sand."[4] This journey ends when Jukes and his horse tumble into a sand-walled pit that serves as a prison for Indians who have been condemned by the custom of their community to live in exile after having been pronounced dead prematurely. Within the "Village of the Dead" at the bottom of the pit there are neither customs nor laws, and Jukes's status as a European means nothing. He is isolated, impotent, and surrounded by hostile strangers: "Here was a Sahib, a representative of the dominant race, helpless as a child and completely at the mercy of his native neighbours" (p. 230). Jukes attempts unsuccessfully to dominate the Indians and make good an escape. Finally, however, he is rescued by a faithful servant who appears miraculously at the top of the pit. Jukes's description of the servant's first words is another indication that his experience has been a dream: the servant calls him "in a whisper—'Sahib! Sahib! Sahib!' exactly as my bearer used to call me in the mornings" (p. 249).

Dream and reality, past, present, and future are all interwoven in Jukes's nightmarish adventure. By comparing his situation to that of a helpless child, Jukes suggests one source of his horrific vision. For his situation in the Village of the Dead is similar to that many imperialists encountered in childhood. Indeed, the similarities between Jukes's experience and that of Punch in "Baa Baa, Black Sheep" are striking. Like Punch, Jukes finds himself alone in a hostile world, tries to adapt by assuming an aggressive facade, fails, and is rescued miraculously only after having lost all hope. For Kipling and many of his fellow imperial servants, the childhood traumas of abandonment seem to have provided the structure and emotional intensity for a vision of India as a similar kind of hell.

But the Village of the Dead also suggests a possible future. By describing the horrific village as a Benthamite republic, Kipling criticizes the relatively liberal elements in the imperial government. In a democratic India, he insists, anarchy would reign. What is worse, the British would be at the mercy of their erstwhile subjects. Thus Jukes's ride takes him into a nightmarish future as well as a haunted past.

Finally, Jukes's vision illuminates his present situation. His life in the pit is not so different from his life in the larger India, where he is isolated in "a desolate sandy stretch of country," surrounded by "coolies . . . neither more nor less exasperating than other gangs" (p. 215), and subject to bouts of delirium-inducing fever. He is trapped in India much as he is in the pit and struggles for survival there while plotting an escape that seems less and less possible. Thus Jukes's nightmare, which is finally that of his creator, combines objective and subjective, contemporary and historical elements. It is at once a devastating illumination of the imperialist's present situation and an exaggeration of that situation caused by projecting onto it past terrors and fears for the future. The power of the nightmare resides in the universality of its sources; everywhere the imperialist turns he sees the same terrible vision of isolation and impotence.

Jukes, who is "not of an imaginative temperament" (p. 236), never apprehends the full significance of his vision. Because he does not connect his brief life in the Village of the Dead with his ongoing life in India, he can continue to operate in that larger hell. But what if he had experienced the dream as a revelation? What if he had recognized the nightmare world and the mundane reality as one? Kipling explores the effect of such a revelation in one of his finest stories, "At the End of the Passage."

The story's most obvious theme is that the imperialist's life in India, far from being idyllic, is hard and bitter. In the story, three young officers gather each weekend at the quarters of a fourth to escape the strain of their daily lives—the surveyor's almost total isolation, the political agent's dangerous situation in a native state, the doctor's hopeless campaign against cholera. Kipling places these figures in the midst of a demonic landscape:

> Four men . . . sat at a table playing whist. The thermometer marked—for them—one hundred and one degrees of heat. The room was darkened till it was only just possible to distinguish the pips of the cards and the very white faces of the players. A tattered, rotten punkah of whitewashed calico was puddling the hot air and whining dolefully at each stroke. Outside lay the gloom of a November day in London. There was neither sky, sun, nor horizon,—nothing but a brown purple haze of heat. It was as though the earth were dying of apoplexy. (p. 328)

Three of the men succeed in maintaining some illusion of normalcy in spite of their situation. They distract themselves by playing cards, singing old songs, and talking of home. But the fourth, their host, Hummil, can no longer find escape in these rituals of distraction. He articulates the truth implicit in Kipling's description of the setting: how can you sing hymns, he demands of his companions, "when you are seven fathom deep in Hell" (p. 342).

Confronted with the truth of his situation, or with what he takes to be the truth, Hummil is breaking down. His insanity takes the form of hallucinations. He imagines "a blind face that cries and can't wipe its eyes, a blind face that chases him down corridors" (p. 352). Menaced by this vision, Hummil reverts to a state of "terrified childhood." Like Punch, Jukes, and the young Kipling, he suffers innocently; although the apparition "has made every night hell" for him, he is "not conscious of having done anything wrong" (p. 350).

There is then, once again, a strong echo of the traumatic childhood experience in this story. But the little world of childhood, the Southsea "House of Desolation" where Kipling lived in terror, is now an entire continent, India, which is described in the story as a "house of torment."

But what does Hummil's hallucinated tormentor represent? Why is it blind, crying, and unable to wipe its eyes? Jonah Raskin suggests that the apparitions Kipling's imperialists encounter are "an image of the self they regularly hide—faces seared, scarred—signifying their inner cynicism and corruption."[5] Raskin's designation of the apparitions as representing the imperialist's true self-image is illuminating, but the image seems to be of the self as innocent victim, not cynical exploiter. Hummil's hallucination projects a terrible insight; he has realized, if only subconsciously, that he himself is blind, terrified, and unable to admit his terror (to wipe away the tears) for fear of being overwhelmed by external enemies or by terror itself. Hummil has seen the true face behind the imperial facade; he has recognized, behind the image of the brave man with the stiff upper lip, the terrified child. And the vision drives him mad.

Thus seeing and insanity are closely identified in "At the End of the Passage." Hummil's madness results, the story suggests, from his insights into his own condition. His assertions—that India is hell and he and his fellows helpless victims—are substantiated by the narrator's description of their situation. Even Hummil's nightmarish tormentor may have a more-than-imagined existence, for the doctor takes a picture of the creature as recorded on Hummil's eye. What Hummil sees, Kipling suggests, is in some sense the truth. It is because he sees more than his fellows that he goes mad.

If the price of vision is madness, perhaps it is better to be blind. Hummil's companions survive by clinging to the distractions and self-deceptions provided in larger imperial communities by the club. Kipling recognizes the value, even the necessity, of such strategies, but he worries that the English retreat to the club has become a rout, and that the security of the Raj is threatened.

Kipling illuminates the crucial function of the clubs in "The Phantom Rickshaw" (1890). Pansay, the protagonist, a heartless lover pursued by hallucinations, takes refuge in the clublike atmosphere of a Simla cafe: "From the horrible to the commonplace is but a step. I tumbled off my horse and dashed, half fainting, into Peliti's for a glass of cherry-brandy. There two or three couples were gathered round the coffee-tables discussing the gossip of the day. Their trivialities were more comforting to me just then than the consolations of religion could have been. I plunged into the midst of the conversation at once."[6] Pansay's flight is from a private demon, but throughout India the club represented a soothing refuge in "the commonplace" from the mysteries and dangers of the larger environment. As an institution dedicated to distraction, it excluded not only the colonized peoples and their culture, but also the unsettling world of controversial ideas. Pansay's comparison of trivial conversation to the "consolations of religion" illuminates the club's unique status as an imperial institution. It offered salvation and security not through a larger vision and deep compassion, but rather by means of an immersion in rituals of triviality, in which neither history nor self need be confronted. To the imperialist, plagued by self-doubt and surrounded by a world in the throes of revolutionary change, this was the obvious escape.

But Kipling looks on the imperialists' plunge into the little world of the club with considerable anxiety. For those characters in his stories who have ventured beyond the commonplace, the club provides little solace; meanwhile it keeps other men from standing firm with their more exposed comrades. Ignorant of India, and addicted to the false security provided by the club, most imperialists are unwilling to take the dangerous but essential step from "the commonplace" to "the horrible." Thus Kipling's genuine appreciation of the distracting and identity-confirming rituals of the club coexists with a recognition that dependence on these rituals only increases the imperialist's vulnerability. This insight is dramatized vividly in "The Return of Imray" (1890).

The three main characters are Imray, an imperial official who has recently disappeared, Strickland, an officer in the imperial police now living in Imray's bungalow, and the narrator, who is staying with Strickland while visiting the district. The story opens with a brief description of the missing Imray. The narrator stresses Imray's conventionality; prior to his disappearance his entire world was the little English community of the station where he lived, and he spent much of his time at the heart of this community, "among the billiard-tables at his Club."[7] For this reason, his disappearance is doubly mysterious.

Strickland's unconventional ways make him Imray's opposite. A favorite Kipling hero in the early stories, Strickland is introduced as a character whom the reader may already know. The narrator alludes specifically to episodes in Strickland's adventurous life, which are chronicled in "Miss Youghal's Sais" (1887) and "The Mark of the Beast" (1890), tales that deal with Strickland's exploits as a master of Indian customs, a cunning impersonator, and a fearless policeman. In spite of his successes, however, Strickland's "investigations into native life" are frowned upon, as are his eccentric domestic habits. The narrator observes that the police officer's "life was sufficiently peculiar, and men complained of his manners and customs" (p. 285). Thus while Imray is portrayed as a model of propriety, Strickland is introduced as a man who meets with disapproval from the members of his own community. Imray relies on the club; Strickland scorns it. Which man, the story asks, should actually command respect and emulation?

The narrator acts as arbiter in resolving this central question. His personality suits him for this role: he knows and admires Strickland, but has a great deal in common with Imray. Their similarity is revealed when the narrator discovers that Strickland's bungalow is haunted: "I explained to Strickland, gently as might be, that I would go over to the Club and find for myself quarters there. I admired his hospitality, was pleased with his guns and rods, but I did not much care for his house and its atmosphere" (p. 292). Strickland opposes this retreat into the conventional in words that have a particular weight of meaning for Kipling: "Stay on . . . and see what this thing means" (p. 292). But the narrator's concern is precisely not to see, and he steadfastly refuses to remain overnight. His instinct, like Imray's, is to seek refuge from mystery within the commonplace world of the club.

The narrator does agree, however, to spend the evening with Strickland, and in the course of his stay the mystery is solved. As events unfold, the dissimilarities between the narrator's responses to the unknown and Strickland's become more and more apparent. When two snakes crawl up into the atticlike space between the ceiling-cloth and the thatched roof, Strickland ignores the narrator's warnings and pursues them. Searching for the snakes, he discovers a bundled object resting on a roof beam. He pushes the mysterious object off onto the ceiling-cloth and it rips through, falling into the room where the narrator is waiting. Once again, the narrator retreats from vision. The bundle lands in front of him. "I dared not look . . . till Strickland . . . was standing by my side" (p. 295). The bundle contains the body of Imray, who, Strickland determines, has been murdered by his servant.

Strickland's boldness enables him to solve a murder that the timid narrator would never even have detected. His victory suggests that other imperial servants must be ready to expose themselves to the threatening world beyond the club and the station. Indeed, the story suggests that such exposure is essential to survival. As it turns out, Imray was killed as a result of an ignorant act of goodwill. He complimented his servant's son, a gesture considered the same as a curse by the boy's people. When the child died of fever, the father killed Imray in revenge. Kipling makes sure that the implications of this tragic misunderstanding won't be lost on his readers: "'Imray made a mistake.' 'Simply and solely through not knowing the nature of the Oriental . . . Bahadur Khan had been with him for four years'" (p. 302). Imray's retreat from exposure to India leaves him fatally ignorant and vulnerable. In contrast, Strickland's habits, for which he is criticized by men like Imray, keep him and the community alive. The immediate political theme is clear: the ignorance fostered by the club represents a dangerous foundation for rule.

In the end, the narrator of "The Return of Imray" signifies his acceptance of this warning by staying on with Strickland in the house of the murdered Imray. But the narrator's close resemblance to the dead man is stressed once again in the final paragraphs of the story. When Strickland observes that Imray's servant had been with him for four years, the narrator is startled: "I shuddered. My own servant had been with me for exactly that length of time" (p. 302).

This insistent identification of the two men coincides with other elements in "The Return of Imray" to invite an interpretation of the story as a loosely constructed psychological allegory. Other aspects of the story that point to this kind of a reading are the vivid and detailed descriptions of the house itself, of the narrator's inexplicable fears, and of the sudden appearance of Imray's body.

Early in the story the reader's attention is directed to the dark and mysterious area of the bungalow just under the roof. "Under the pitch of the roof ran a ceiling-cloth which looked just as neat as a white-washed ceiling. The landlord had repainted it when Strickland took the bungalow. Unless you knew how Indian bungalows were built you would never have suspected that above the cloth lay the dark three-cornered cavern of the roof, where the beams and the underside of the thatch harboured all manner of rats, bats, ants, and foul things" (p. 287). Among the "foul things" hidden away in this carefully screened-off realm is the body of Imray, whose ghost, like an unacknowledged fear, so frightens the narrator in the room below. In contrast to the narrator, Strickland is not afraid. Like a modern-day psychoanalyst, he fearlessly explores the dark world that is the source of the narrator's fears, while the narrator himself remains below, insisting on his total ignorance of what lies above while, at the same time, manifesting an inordinate degree of anxiety. "I set my teeth and lifted the rod," he recalls, "for I had not the least knowledge of what might descend" (p. 294).

When Imray's body falls, the narrator experiences the event as a traumatic psychological breakthrough, the emergence into consciousness of some hitherto repressed terror. The mysterious object breaks through the fragile barrier of cloth with a terrible, dreamlike slowness and inexorability: "I saw the ceiling-cloth nearly in the centre of the room bag with a shape that was pressing it downwards and downwards towards the lighted lamp on the table. I snatched the lamp out of danger and stood back. Then the cloth ripped out from the walls, tore, split, swayed, and shot down upon the table something that I dared not look at till Strickland had slid down the ladder and was standing by my side." (p. 295). Why does the narrator experience the event in this way; why is he so terrified by the bundle that he dares not face it? The reiterated identification of the narrator with Imray provides a possible answer. Perhaps Imray's body, like the terrible apparition that forces its way into Hummil's vision in "At the End of the Passage," represents the narrator's own repressed self-image, an image of himself as a potential victim of forces beyond his knowledge.

Indeed, Kipling's descriptions of madness during this period often involve the breakthrough of sinister forces from a realm of outer darkness. The narrator of "The Phantom Rickshaw" explains Pansay's death with the theory "that there was a crack in Pansay's head and a little bit of the Dark World came through and pressed him to death."[8] Although Hummil's madness in "At the End of the Passage" is attributed to his having fallen into the "Dark Places,"[9] the fact that the ceiling-cloth of his bungalow is torn is mentioned twice. But while for Pansay and Hummil the breakthroughs prove fatal, the narrator in "The Return of Imray" is cured of his terror by the appearance of Imray. This is true, however, only because Strickland is there to confront his fears with him, to provide a logical explanation of their source, and to offer a prescription for their permanent banishment.

The allegorical and literal elements of the story merge at this point. Kipling is concerned to show that the narrator's fear is somewhat irrational, and his reaction to that fear totally so. Imray's ghost, which has plagued the narrator, is in one sense a projection of his own fears. But it is a projection founded on an actual murder — Imray and thousands of other imperial servants have been killed in India. These murders, Kipling suggests, provide the fertile soil in which the fears of living imperialists can flourish. Thus the images of men actually killed in India find their ways into the unconsciousness of their living fellows, where they survive as foreshadowings of potential doom. The flight to the club results from this combination of real dangers and imagined horrors.

What Strickland shows the narrator is that his future need not be Imray's, that the dreams that haunt his sleep do not depict an inevitable doom. Imray, he insists, died because he was ignorant; his death could have been avoided. Only if the narrator follows Imray's course and withdraws into the club is he likely to meet his fate. Kipling's theme here is clear: he invites the imperial servant to become more familiar with the Indian community, and he argues that the fear preventing exploration of that community is the imperialist's greatest enemy.

Although the presence of deeply-felt insecurity in the imperial official's personality represents for Kipling a flaw in the imperial mold, he suggests that in other members of the imperial service such feelings may be useful. Specifically, he sees self-doubt and fear of freedom as resources for the maintenance of discipline among the masses of soldiers. What represents a painful weakness in an officer is a virtue of sorts in his men, or so Kipling suggests in "The Madness of Private Ortheris" (1888).

In this story from *Soldiers Three*, Ortheris's "madness" takes the form of a compulsion to desert the Indian Army. This impulse is mad for two reasons: first, because Ortheris is only four months from being sent home and, second, because to an army man desertion represents both a crime and a dishonor. Yet Ortheris's reasons for wishing to desert are basically sound. He expresses his homesickness eloquently: "I'm sick for London again; sick for the sounds of 'er, an' the sights of 'er, and the stinks of 'er; orange-peel and hasphalte an' gas comin' in over Vaux'all Bridge."[10] But his larger longing is for autonomy: "No bloomin' guard-mountin', no bloomin' rotten-stone, nor Khaki, an' yourself your own master" (p. 25). A fierce social bitterness complements these painful personal emotions: "There's the Widder sittin' at 'Ome with a gold crownd on 'er 'ead; and 'ere am Hi, Stanley Orth'ris, the Widder's property, a rottin' FOOL!" (p. 25). Ortheris's madness, as is often the case in Kipling, stems not from his being out of touch with his situation, but from a too-clear apprehension of it.

Private Mulvaney and the unnamed narrator, appalled at Ortheris's condition, set out to "cure" him. Mulvaney admits sadly that he can do little for Ortheris: "I've bruk his head . . . time an' agin. I've nearly kilt him wid the belt, an' *yet* I can't knock thim fits out av his soft head" (p. 29). Physical coercion, the only disciplinary tool Mulvaney has at his command, will not work. The narrator's method is more subtle. He contrives to get Ortheris into civilian clothes, and to leave him alone for almost two hours. In this brief period the cure is effected. When Mulvaney and the narrator return they find that "the devils had departed from Private Stanley Ortheris, No. 22639 B Company. The loneliness, the dusk, and the waiting had driven them out, as I had hoped. We set off at the double and found him plunging about wildly through the grass, with his coat off—my coat off, I mean. He was calling for us like a madman" (p. 29). Although the devils are said to have departed, Ortheris is still behaving like a madman; his "insane" desire for freedom has been exorcised by the conjuring up of an even stronger demon, that of isolation. By leaving Ortheris alone without the insignia of his old identity, the narrator dramatizes for him a negative definition of freedom as isolation, nothingness. Ortheris, already plagued as a soldier by a sense of his insignificance, reacts as the narrator expects he will, by surrendering all hope of freedom and accepting his slavery once again.

Kipling suggests the nature of the cure by his elaborate naming of Ortheris: "Private Stanley Ortheris, No. 22639, B Company." Unable to endure aloneness without support, or to find positive support in his search for freedom, Ortheris steps back into the framework of an authoritarian organization, and his personal identity, his name, is precisely framed within signs of rank and group. His madness now stems from his need to regain this demeaning security as quickly as possible. Where he had once dreamed of never wearing khaki again, he now rushes to put on his old uniform, and the narrator observes with casual precision that "the rasp of his own 'grayback' shirt and the squeak of his boots seemed to bring him to himself" (p. 30). For this is literally what occurs; Ortheris's "self" is the space within the uniform, a constricting, painful, but well-defined identity.

Ortheris seals his return to sanity with one last illuminating act of madness. He gives his belt to Mulvaney, and invites the man to beat him with it. Yet this act is consistent with his purpose. For physical pain administered by an external authority can have a satisfying effect on an individual terrified of isolation. Like the rasp of the shirt, the pain of the belt ratifies Ortheris's return to an accustomed role, to a community of men whose purpose is to give pain to one another and for whom the bestowing of pain has become almost an act of affection. For as Kipling observes in a poem written many years later, "Hymn to Physical Pain," this kind of suffering can provide desperate distraction from vaster agonies of the spirit and imagination—just the agonies Ortheris is fleeing.

Significantly, the narrator of the story has no scruples about using Ortheris's deepest weakness to manipulate him back into his socially assigned place. To some degree the narrator's callous action may be justified. Ortheris will be sent home soon, and he and his fellow soldiers have been transformed by their experiences into deeply dependent beings. But other, less exploitative types of mutual dependency were available to working-class men in Ortheris's day, and the narrator's complacency and his pride at having driven Ortheris back into terror and thence to slavery, are unpleasant. He humiliates Ortheris deeply, more deeply than Ortheris himself recognizes, without expressing any criticism of the institutions that rendered the soldier so pathetically vulnerable to manipulation. Kipling seems to share this complacency.

Thus "The Madness of Private Ortheris," when compared with the other stories discussed in this chapter, reveals a cruel double standard in Kipling's thinking. In the other stories Kipling describes imprinted fears of isolation and inadequacy as the afflictions they are. Moreover, he proposes ways of mitigating these terrors and encouraging greater self-reliance. Yet when he turns from depicting the men of his own class to those of a lower one, his attitude changes. Then the internalized fears and doubts are enlisted, with the author's approval, to drive a man dreaming of freedom back into a cruelly restrictive mold. Autonomy, it appears, is to be reserved for the lucky few. For the rest, the nightmares of abandonment and inadequacy are to be nurtured and employed as internalized allies of social control, like soldiers in a conquered country. What Kipling ignores in endorsing this treatment of the common soldier is the fact that he and his fellow upper servants of Empire are also soldiers, and may also need to be kept in line. They too are likely to dream of flight back to England or establishment of quasi-feudal autonomy in India, and it is not likely that their superiors will hesitate to employ the same methods of control against them that they themselves use against their own inferiors.

While most of Kipling's imperialists retreat from contact with India into the illusory refuge of the club or the rigid supports of army life, a small minority are tempted in the opposite direction, toward total immersion in the Indian community. Kipling portrays these men sympathetically, but judges their course to be as disastrous as that of the majority. By identifying with Indians and exposing themselves so completely to India, they also render themselves vulnerable. And total exposure, like total withdrawal, makes domination impossible. Kipling's judgment in this instance has important ramifications for his role as an imperial artist, since the impulse to imaginative identification is one an artist can hardly afford to stifle if he is to render character convincingly.

Why are some men moved to immerse themselves in the Indian community? Trejago, the British protagonist of "Beyond the Pale" (1888), crosses the dangerous border in search of knowledge and passion. His curiosity leads him to investigate Indian culture and the Indian commuity. His wanderings take him "deep away in the heart of the City,"[11] where he encounters Bisesa, a lovely young Indian widow. Thus Trejago begins "a double life." He endures the daytime routine of work and social obligation, only to slip away at night to Bisesa's cell, the room in her uncle's house where she waits for Trejago. His life with her is idyllic, and he grows to love her "more than any one else in the world."[12] At the deepest level, it seems, Bisesa and her community represent to Trejago and Kipling a world of unfettered passion in which the emotional and sensual inhibitions of English civilization can be set aside.

In "To Be Filed for Reference" (1888) another imperial official, McIntosh Jellaludin, immerses himself even more completely than Trejago in the Indian community. Driven by drink and a desire for knowledge, Jellaludin openly deserts the English community. He marries an Indian woman, adopts the Mohammedan faith, and lives for seven years among the Indians. These actions are brought on by Jellaludin's dreams of omnipotence and anarchic irresponsibility: "I am as the Gods," Jellaludin boasts, "knowing good and evil, but untouched by either."[13]

Trejago and Jellaludin, created by Kipling during his years as a journalist in India, succumb to temptations he seems to have experienced himself. C. E. Carrington stresses Kipling's fascination with the Indian community. The young newspaperman, he writes, was reputed to know more about the low life of Lahore than the police, and to be seriously studying the Indian underworld.[14] Like the decadents and naturalists, his artistic contemporaries in Europe, Kipling was not concerned primarily with "respectable" poverty, but rather with the anarchic life of the streets and alleys. In *Something of Myself* he describes his night wanderings in Lahore: "I would wander till dawn in all manner of odd places—liquor-shops, gambling- and opium-dens, which are not a bit mysterious, wayside entertainments such as puppet-shows, native dances; or in and about the narrow gullies under the Mosque of Wazir Khan for the sheer sake of looking."[15]

But Kipling was after more than a glimpe of the exotic; he wanted to get to know the Indian people themselves in order to write about their lives. Indeed, he had determined that his first novel would be about the Eurasian community. Yet although many of his early stories and sketches clearly draw on his own experiences across the cultural border, the major work was never completed. Kipling's immersion in the Indian community seems never to have progressed far beyond such excursions as the ones described above. The routes taken by Trejago and Jellaludin were avoided by their creator.

It is not surprising, then, that the stories of these two men who do make fundamental breaks with orthodox ideas and behavior end tragically. From the beginning of "Beyond the Pale" the narrator warns the reader of the foolishness of Trejago's actions: "A man should, whatever happens, keep to his own caste, race and breed. Let the White go to the White and the Black to the Black. Then, whatever trouble falls is in the ordinary course of things—neither sudden, alien nor unexpected. This is the story of a man who wilfully stepped beyond the safe limits of decent everyday society, and paid for it heavily."[16]

There is an undertone of parody here, especially in the phrase "decent everyday society," with its insistence on the mundane and domestic. Perhaps, as Louis Cornell suggests, Kipling is preparing the reader to recognize the superiority of passionate, mysterious India.[17] But the last words in the passage lack the mocking tone of what has preceded, and the final "heavily" casts an ominous shadow over the whole. Indeed, the story, as it unwinds, does tend to confirm the narrator's injunctions. After a month of bliss, Bisesa and Trejago's secret liaison is discovered by her uncle. Trejago is wounded in the groin, Bisesa's hands are cut off, and the window of her cell is walled over. Thus Trejago learns that in the world of passion beyond the law, hatred as well as love is unbounded. And his passionate exposure to India ends in the wounding of his very capacity for passion.

Kipling clearly sympathizes with Trejago, and longs for the freedom from conventional restraints that he so briefly attains. I disagree with Cornell, however, when he argues that "Kipling sees around his narrator and lets us know that the reporter is wrong, that we are not to accept his cautious warnings, that Bisesa and the world she represents are worth the terrible risks Trejago has run."[18] Rather, it seems to me that Kipling's voice and the narrator's are one, and that he is issuing himself as well as the audience a warning, dramatizing the consequences of a too complete exposure to India. Trejago's punishment is, implicitly, castration; isolated and exposed by his enthrallment to the dream of passionate freedom in India, he fails to protect himself against its dangers and so loses his power.

Thus the narrator's mocking tone does not point, I believe, to any fundamental rebellion. Like so many Kipling figures, the narra-

Strickland

tor combines a superficial appearance of irreverence with a deeper commitment to the program of the authorities. The tone reflects only Kipling's dilemma: he is unprepared to risk exposing himself to isolation or to alien worlds, but he is uneasily aware of the desiccating restrictions of his own world. Out of this dilemma comes not only the mockery, which is to some extent self-mockery, but also the perverse call for self-limitation. Trejago, the narrator insists, "knew too much in the first instance; and he saw too much in the second. He took too deep an interest in native life; but he will never do so again."[19]

Jellaludin's punishment, like his transgression, is more severe than Trejago's. Having shifted over, mind and body, to the Indian side of the border, he pays for his apostasy with his life. There are three main characters in the story, the unnamed narrator, Jellaludin, and Strickland, the hero of "The Return of Imray." The narrator closely resembles Kipling himself. A young Englishman, apparently a writer, he enjoys exploring the bazaars and caravanserai. But in spite of his habits and profession he retains, like Kipling, a healthy regard for the opinions of his peers. Concerned to maintain his respectability, he will only visit Jellaludin at night: "One cannot visit a loafer in the Serai by day. Friends buying horses would not understand it."[20]

By his public act of immersion in the Indian community Jellaludin has put all such considerations of social acceptability behind him. He no longer needs to concern himself with the restraints imposed by the conventional wisdom of the British community, and he has gained a knowledge of India that no man shackled by such restraints could hope to attain. He mocks Strickland, the model of the knowledgeable Anglo-Indian in several Kipling stories, as an ignorant man, and boasts that the book he is writing, *Mother Maturin*, will reveal more about the Indian way of life than any previous work. (Kipling's novel of Indian life, with which he had been struggling for several years at the time he wrote this story, was to be entitled *Mother Maturin*.) But before he can complete his masterwork, Jellaludin pays for the knowledge he has gained with his life. Wracked by drink and disease, without the civilized protections of warm clothing and medicine, he dies in his squalid hut. Far from achieving his dream of godlike freedom, he has become the slave of poverty, the victim of an exposure signified at a literal level by the lack of blankets on his palet. The route of the greatest exposure and exploration, Kipling suggests, does not lead to the greatest license and power.

Significantly, it is at this point in the story, after Jellaludin's death, that Strickland actually appears. The narrator turns to him for his judgment of Jellaludin's work, thus giving the victim of Jellaludin's mockery the final word. There is an interesting similarity in this sense between the plot of "To Be Filed For Reference" and that of "The Return of Imray." In both stories the narrator becomes the arbiter of a conflict between two men representing different ways of dealing with India. In both cases one of these men is Strickland, and in both cases he emerges as the wiser. Yet while in one case he represents the course of greater exposure, in the other his is the more conservative course.

The contrast between Strickland's life style and Jellaludin's reveals the limited nature of the exposure and autonomy advocated by Kipling. Jellaludin's complete and public transfer of allegiance, his identification with India, isolates and destroys him. Strickland, on the other hand, crosses the border only in disguise and only to do the bidding of the imperial authorities. He intentionally minimizes his physical, psychological, and emotional exposure, and never commits himself, like Jellaludin, to share the Indians' burdens along with their knowledge. As a result, he achieves a certain spurious autonomy, for he is free to move at will from culture to culture and is bound by the conventional restraints of neither. He, not Jellaludin, achieves the authoritarian version of freedom, the liberation at once from social restrictions, from the anxiety of powerless isolation, and from questions of moral responsibility. He experiences the joy of knowing without the pain of being known. For these reasons, "Natives hated Strickland; but they were afraid of him."[21] And for these same reasons, he is Kipling's ideal.

The titles of Kipling's stories are frequently double entendres. Jellaludin's tale is "To Be Filed For Reference" not only as a reminder

of who wrote *Mother Maturin*, but also, perhaps, as a warning to
Kipling himself against taking a similar route. This warning may
explain why Kipling's *Mother Maturin* was never finished. Kipling
seems to have decided finally that the sympathetic immersion necessary to create such a work was too risky, that India could only be
encountered in a mode of physical and emotional aloofness no less
rigorous, if somewhat more flexible, than that represented by the
club. A novel whose main characters were to be Eurasians could
hardly be written from such a perspective.

Kipling's early work suggests that his initial impulse was indeed toward exposure, exploration, and identification, but
that this impulse was soon stifled. Throughout his writing career
Kipling creates Indian characters and describes their motivations,
but only in his earlier stories, those of the eighties, does he create
sympathetic Indian characters who do not conform to orthodox imperial assumptions. The good Indians of the later stories either respect the British or criticize anti-imperialist elements in English society; the rest are fools or villains.

Yet one of Kipling's earliest published stories is a sympathetic
portrayal of an Indian woman who rebels against her British superiors. "Lispeth" (1886) is about an Indian girl who becomes the pro-
tégée of Christian missionaries. Her own people ostracize her for
adopting Western habits and values, but she endures this treatment
gladly and grows every day in wisdom and knowledge. Then, having rescued an English traveler, she falls in love with him. She determines to marry the man, and neither he nor the missionaries have
the decency to disillusion her. Only months after he has left does
the chaplain's wife reveal the truth: "That the Englishman had only
promised his love to keep her quiet—that he had never meant anything, and that it was wrong and improper of Lispeth to think of
marriage with an Englishman, who was of superior clay."[22] Her illusions of British good faith and fraternity shattered, Lispeth rebels:
" 'I am going back to my own people,' said she. 'You have killed
Lispeth. There is only left old Jadéh's daughter . . . You are all
liars, you English.' "[23]

Within the bounds of the story, there is nothing to contradict the justice of Lispeth's condemnation of the British, or to challenge her right to make it. Kipling insists on the truth of her original commitment to Western ideals, celebrates her love for the Englishman, sympathizes with her trust, and respects her reaction into traditionalism. Imperialism's promise to educate the colonized for equality is revealed as a hollow sham. Yet Kipling may not have intended so broad a criticism of imperial practice as I suggest. Significantly, the Englishmen on whom Lispeth bases her generalized condemnation belong to groups disliked by many imperialists and frequently criticized by Kipling: missionaries and tourists. Moreover, in later years Kipling attacks reformers for encouraging expectations of equality among the Indians. He argues that such promises are unrealistic and should not be made. But if this is his theme in "Lispeth," it is almost completely obscured by his admiration for the girl and his clear insistence on her superiority to her English guardians. Thus early in his writing career Kipling describes the imperial situation as seen by a betrayed and righteously indignant victim of the British.

Another early story in which Kipling identifies himself for a time with a perspective critical of imperial ideology is "His Chance in Life" (1887). The story begins with disquisition on the racial heritage of Eurasians, "the Borderline folk" in whom "the Black and the White mix very quaintly. . . . Sometimes the White shows in spurts of fierce, childish pride—which is Pride of Race run crooked—and sometimes the Black in still fiercer abasement and humility, half heathenish customs and strange, unaccountable impulses to crime."[24] But the succeeding paragraphs appear to challenge the substance and pontifical tone of this first statement. The narrator questions the capacity of Europeans to understand the Eurasian consciousness: "One of these days, this people . . . will turn out a writer or a poet; and then we shall know how they live and what they feel. In the meantime, any stories about them cannot be absolutely correct in fact or inference" (pp. 84–85). As if to demonstrate this point, he opens the story with an example of European blindness: "Miss Vezzis came from across the Borderline to look after some children who belonged to a lady until a regularly ordained

nurse could come out. The lady said Miss Vezzis was a bad, dirty
nurse and inattentive. It never struck her that Miss Vezzis had her
own life to lead and her own affairs to worry over, and that these
affairs were the most important things in the world to Miss Vezzis.
Very few mistresses admit this sort of reasoning" (p. 85). These two
observations on the lack of understanding, the generalization and
the concrete example, appear to be setting the stage for a major revelation of the problems arising from the imperialists' assumption of
rectitude.

Instead, as the story unfolds, the conventional ideology of racial
superiority quickly reestablishes its control over the narrator's consciousness. The story portrays the efforts of Michele D'Cruze, "a
poor, sickly weed and very black" to win Miss Vezzis. D'Cruze and
she are betrothed, but her family will not allow them to marry until
he is earning at least fifty rupees a month, and this seems an impossible condition. Then, while serving as government telegraph oper-
ator in a small town, D'Cruze finds himself the ranking official
present when a religious riot breaks out. He meets the challenge,
puts down the riot, and maintains control until the English arrive.
At that point, unfortunately, he dissolves into a mild hysteria, but
the understanding imperial official sees to it that he is rewarded
with a better post, one that earns him sixty-five rupees a month.

The story focuses on the motivations behind D'Cruze's courageous actions. According to the narrator, two basic impulses determine his response: he has some white blood in his veins, and he is
madly in love. These impulses to heroism are reinforced later on
when "he had tasted for the first time Responsibility and Success"
(p. 90), but fundamentally D'Cruze's heroism is, in the narrator's
eyes, an anomaly. Credit for it rests not with him as an individual,
but with his one European ancestor and the god of love. D'Cruze's
reaction to the arrival of an English officer is intepreted as a sign of
his basic inferiority:

> In the presence of this young Englishman, Michele felt himself slip-
> ping back more and more into the native; and the tale of the Tibasu
> Riots ended, with the strain on the teller, in an hysterical outburst

of tears, bred by sorrow that he had killed a man, shame that he could not feel as uplifted as he had felt through the night, and childish anger that his tongue could not do justice to his great deeds. It was the White drop in Michele's veins dying out, though he did not know it. (p. 91)

What has really died out here is the narrator's saving recognition that cross-cultural understanding is extremely difficult and that simplistic formulas imposed from without are more likely to distort than to illuminate the state of things across the border. The narrator, ignoring his own warnings, claims that he knows what motivates Michele, even though the man himself is ignorant.

Why should Kipling so betray his own best insights? Perhaps because these insights threaten his identity as an Englishman and an imperialist. Kipling seems to be trying, in this story, to have it both ways—to enter sympathetically into the consciousness of a colonized person, and to maintain his allegiance to the racial suppositions of imperialism. But the first endeavor draws him inexorably towards subversion. His recognition of a unique Eurasian perspective leads him to scrutinize carefully at least some Englishmen's criticisms of the people they dominate. And his description of a Eurasian's success at maintaining social order calls into question the fundamental English assumption that the colonized peoples cannot look after themselves. To diffuse these potentially dangerous insights, Kipling quickly turns to the depiction of an imperialist, the young officer, who does understand, and to a pseudo-scientific explanation of D'Cruze's actions, which robs them of any political significance.

The story also contains two less obvious but equally subversive insights. The first is that D'Cruze responds positively to the taste of "Responsibility and Success." This is a taste that imperialism has systematically denied to the colonized peoples, on the grounds that they were incapable of appreciating it. The second, even more compromising observation, is that it is only when a European appears that Michele breaks down. Kipling's explanation of this breakdown is blatantly inadequate. Even if the theory of racial blood is accepted, why should Michele's "White drop" recede at the moment of the European's arrival? Kipling's first description of D'Cruze's

reaction is more illuminating. The man, Kipling writes, "felt himself slipping back more and more into the native." What Kipling
renders here, with impressive clarity, is the operation of the racial
stereotype that the imperialists worked so hard to establish. Alone
in the village, D'Cruze operates successfully as a man. Confronted
with a white face, he recalls that his identity, originally imposed
but long since internalized, is not that of a man but that of a "native," an inferior being. As a result, he slips back into that role.
Kipling hurries to obscure the true nature of this process by explaining it in "scientific" terms, but he has already revealed the workings
of the machinery of domination.

Finally, then, Kipling's unwillingness to risk isolating himself
from the orthodox imperial community thwarts his efforts to
achieve illuminating identification with the colonized peoples.
D'Cruze's victory must be denied him, safely subsumed within the
categories of racial superiority. Thus the opportunity for discovery
is lost. Kipling will continue to describe Indians from without, and
in some cases will put words in their mouths with convincing tone
and feeling. But when deeper explanations are due, when it comes
time to explore behind the masks of the conventional roles and definitions, he will remain faithful to the official dogmas of reactionary
imperialism.

James Fitzjames Stephen, Leslie's brother and a high official in the
Indian administration, described that administration in 1883 as

> an absolute government, founded not on consent, but on conquest.
> It does not represent the native principles of life or of government,
> and it can never do so until it represents heathenism and barbarism.
> It represents a belligerent civilization, and no anomaly can be more
> striking or so dangerous, as its administration by men, who being
> at the head of a Government founded upon conquest, implying at
> every point the superiority of the conquering race, of their ideas,
> their institutions, their opinions and their principles, and having no
> justification for its existence except that superiority, shrink from
> the open, uncompromising, straightforward assertion of it.[25]

Stephen's description clarifies Kipling's situation. The India to
which he returned in 1882 was a country under occupation, and the

kind of communication he sought at first to establish with the Indian people would have involved real physical and social risks. Instead of taking these risks, Kipling retreated, not only from the reality of India but from the painfully exposed social and psychological position most modern artists have endured. Perhaps because his own early experience of isolation and hostility had been so great, he chose to enlist his energies in the service of that "belligerent civilization" celebrated by Stephen, and to project its values and vision in his work. As an artist, then, Kipling assumes the same relation to the Indian people that he celebrates in his hero Strickland. He infiltrates the Indian community as a secret agent of imperialism, exposing himself just enough to gain the knowledge needed to give his reductive and distorted portraits of the Indians the semblance of adequacy and authenticity.

3

LIFTING THE BURDEN:
KIPLING IN THE NINETIES

*India was awake, and Kim was in the middle of it, more awake and
excited than any one.*

KIPLING, Kim

Kipling returned to England in 1889 and quickly became a
literary celebrity. He continued to write about India, but in a
manner that reflects his new perspective. The India depicted in the
fiction of the 1890s is a more benign and less complicated place than
the old, stubbornly problematic India. Underlying this apparent
transformation, however, is a deeper continuity of purpose. Kipling's fiction continues to focus on the burdens and responsibilities
of the imperial ruler. In the eighties this concern involves Kipling in
the diagnosis of imperial problems; in the nineties he offers his plan
for perfecting the imperial mold.

During the nineties Kipling wrote four long books on the theme
of education: *The Jungle Book, Captains Courageous, Stalky and Co.,*
and *Kim* (which was not published until 1901). One source of Kipling's interest in this theme was almost certainly his desire to erase
imaginatively the memory of his own terrible childhood. But this
concern with education has a more public dimension as well. Kipling realized during his years in India that he and his fellow imperial
servants had been psychologically crippled by their upbringing. He
realized, too, that this crippling affected their ability to rule. Now,
having analyzed the problem and illuminated its source in a trau-

matic series of abandonments, Kipling set out to present his blue-
prints for change, his picture of the ideal educational program for
the imperial officer and of the ideal officer's new relationship with
the subject community.

The imperial dilemma, as identified by Kipling in the eighties, resides in the problems created by the policies of abandonment and
aloofness. On the one hand, Kipling accepts the necessity of abandonment in the form of early exile from home and family. He does
so on the supposition that the "sheltered life system" of education
insures only that the young imperial servant will be unequal to the
inevitable shock of exposure his vocation entails.[1] On the other
hand, however, Kipling knows from bitter experience the terrible
effect of early banishment to England and the English public school
system. The need, as he defines it in the works of the nineties, is for
an abandonment that does not break the young spirit but, rather,
strengthens and expands it.

Just as Kipling accepts the need for some form of abandonment,
he also argues that the imperial rulers must remain somewhat aloof
from their Indian subjects. In several stories he demonstrates the
utility of aloofness, which provides the imperial ruler with a protective aura of mystery and superiority and allows him to monopolize
the strategies and instruments of rule. But, at the same time, Kipling insists in other stories that too much aloofness only wraps the
imperialist in ignorance, thus undermining his ability to rule. Furthermore, the conventional modes of aloofness impose unbearable
constraints on the imperialist by forcing him to live like a beseiged
alien in the land he nominally dominates. Clearly, officers in the
field must be endowed with the spirit and skills necessary to break
out into the larger community. When they possess this ability,
Kipling suggests in the fiction of the nineties, imperial domination
will be secure.

Strickland, Kipling's ideal imperial officer in the early stories,
comes close to achieving this goal. By internalizing aloofness
through a series of psychological and technical ploys, he is able to
move freely among the Indian people, collecting information useful
to the Raj while enjoying considerable freedom from the restric-

tions imposed within the British community. But Kipling occasionally suggests that even Strickland is too much of an alien: "Strickland hates being mystified by natives, because his business in life is to overmatch them with their own weapons. He had not yet succeeded in doing this, but in fifteen or twenty years he will have made some small progress."[2] Strickland remains a model of excellence in the nineties, but Kipling makes it clear that the days of his supremacy are numbered. The new generation of rulers, if properly fostered, will surpass even him.

Their supremacy can be assured, Kipling insists, by means of a single revision in the imperial program of education. Instead of being exiled to the society of the dominant community—that is, to England—the young Anglo-Indian should be raised in India and exposed to its society, to the community of the subject peoples. If this is done, Kipling suggests in *The Jungle Book, Kim,* and several stories, future imperialists will not harbor a crippling conviction of their own inadequacy, nor will they spend their lives in fear and ignorance of their subjects. The benefits of abandonment and aloofness will be preserved, their dangers eliminated.

Kipling's new heroes have the benefit of this program of education. Confident, adventurous youths and men, they are in many ways extremely attractive. The spirit in which Kipling portrays them is equally so, for it is one of celebration and contrasts sharply with the cynicism and despair of the earlier tales. But, finally, the new program is made credible, its goals acceptable, only by major acts of distortion. To create the situation required by the educational and political program he envisions, Kipling must distort both the realities of social relationships and the historical situation in India. What he is attempting is no less than the removal of conflict and fear from one of the most conflict-ridden situations imaginable, the domination of one people by another. Because his goal is so unrealistic, his pursuit of it leads him further and further from the dark but powerful realism of his earliest works, deeper and deeper into fantasy. Moreover, his quest brings him very close to sedition, for his perfect ruler, the white man born and bred in India, demands a degree of autonomy incompatible with the system of an imperial state.

The journey into fantasy begins with *The Jungle Book* (1894), a collection of stories about beasts who act like men and about the Indian boy who becomes their ruler. The book functions, among other things, as a fable of imperial education and rule, with Mowgli behaving toward the beasts as the British do to the Indians. By turning the subject community into a community of animals, and by exploring the problems of ruling them through the vehicle of the beast fable, Kipling makes his educational and political programs seem more plausible and just than they actually are.

The Jungle Book opens with Mowgli's abandonment. Threatened by the tiger Shere Khan, the child's parents flee, leaving him at the mercy of the jungle. Like the Anglo-Indian Punch in "Baa Baa, Black Sheep" when he is first exiled to England, Mowgli does not recognize his jeopardy. He laughs when Father Wolf checks his deadly spring in midair, and brazenly forces his way past Mother Wolf's cubs to her teats. This boldness on Mowgli's part seems certain to provoke an even harsher reaction than did Punch's. But because Mowgli, unlike Punch, has been exiled into a community ultimately less powerful than his own, he remains unscathed. Fearing retribution and proud to possess a human child, the wolves cautiously nourish and protect Mowgli.

Not only the wolves but the larger jungle community as well give shelter to the abandoned child. Because Mowlgi joins the jungle society as a wolf, he has little to fear from its other inhabitants. (Had he been adopted by the antelopes, for instance, it would have been harder for Kipling to ignore the degree of anxiety and the amount of carnage licensed by his Social Darwinian Jungle Law.) Moreover, the child is quickly singled out for favor by some of the jungle's most powerful citizens, Baloo, the wise bear, Bagheera, the panther, and Kaa, the python. These allies, the magical helpers of Kipling's fairy tale, provide Mowgli not only with support and approval, but also with the words and signs that make the other beasts his allies. When, for instance, Mowgli finds himself threatened by cobras, he gives the Snake's call, "We be of one blood, ye and I," and they honor his claim to kinship.

Thus instead of experiencing loneliness and impotence as Punch does in powerful, uncaring England, Mowgli comes rapidly to feel at home in the midst of his vast jungle family. This is possible, Kipling suggests, because Mowgli is a man among beasts, and so a representative of a dominant race. The wolves protect Mowgli because they recognize that humans are powerful creatures who must be respected: "Man-killing means, sooner or later, the arrival of white men on elephants, with guns. . . . Then everybody in the jungle suffers."[3] (The parallel with imperial policies of reprisal is obvious.) Also, because humans are so powerful, to be identified with them confers a certain status: "Now," says Mother Wolf, "was there ever a wolf that could boast of a man's cub among her children" (p. 6). Moreover, because Mowgli is a man among beasts he possesses, even as a child, traits and tools that he can use to thwart any enemies. When Shere Khan the tiger and the wolves turn on him, Mowgli subdues them with fire, a weapon only man has learned to use. Because he possesses such weapons, Mowgli does not experience impotence, nor does he develop habits of dependency. Instead, the trials he undergoes in exile confirm his self-confidence and independence.

Mowgli's ability to take revenge on his enemies is especially stressed. Kipling suggests that this ability is necessary to the development of a healthy personality. After describing one act of vengeance, for instance, he writes that "the pleasantest part of Mowgli's life began. He had the good conscience that comes from paying debts" (p. 219). Kipling is right in suggesting that impotence breeds bitterness and even guilt, but Mowgli's acts of massive retaliation seem more heinous than the injustices which provoke them. In razing an Indian village, for example, Mowgli uses his power not as the confident young hero he is supposed to be would use it, but as such power might be used by a vindictive victim of prolonged humiliation. He uses it, in other words, as Punch or Kipling himself might have, after their years of tormenting impotence. Thus in this and several other instances, the impulses of the maimed author seem to poison the spirit of a hero whom he intends to endow with perfect psychological health.

To be above yet to belong, to be obeyed as a god and loved as a brother, this is Kipling's dream for the imperial ruler, a dream that Mowgli achieves. The roots of such a desire can be found in the authoritarian's appetite for absolute power and for external support, and in the infantile dream of power without responsibility. The structure of the British imperial system, like that of all authoritarian systems, reflected those needs; the individual took his place in a hierarchy of power, behaving as a subordinate to his superiors, a comrade to his fellows, and a master to his Indian subjects. But the imperialist's comrades often lived hours away, and his subjects were so numerous and strange that he hardly felt himself their master. Thus from an authoritarian point of view his situation was far from ideal.

The lot of the imperial officer in the field would improve immensely, *The Jungle Book* suggests, if the new program it recommends were carried out. The first of the three authoritarian relationships, that of the individual as slave to his masters, would be almost totally abolished. Because Mowgli has been so utterly abandoned by his own community, he feels neither responsible to it nor dependent on it. He is autonomous. As for the second relationship, that of the individual as brother to his fellows, that would be fused with the third — the individual as master to his subjects. Mowgli lives surrounded by brothers who are also servants, enjoying at once the gratifications of fraternal support and those of absolute authority. Purged of the need for dependency and free of the institutions that enforce it, he knows the pleasures of domination in their purest form.

In the final story of *The Jungle Book* Mowgli becomes a forest-guard, thus assuming a role analogous from Kipling's point of view to that of the imperial district officer, though one step further down the hierarchical ladder of communities. Unlike the typical imperial officer, however, Mowgli comes to his work already familiar with the community he is to rule, and ready to live in its midst. As Mowgli's name, "the Frog," implies, his felicitous abandonment has made him a uniquely amphibious creature, at home in both the human and the jungle worlds. Neither the claustrophobic walls of mud and prejudice that he encounters in the Indian village nor the limited powers and perspectives of the jungle community can constrain him. Instead, he lives unbound between the two communities, taking what he needs from each in the manner of a licensed border bandit. Even Bagheera, a prince of the jungle, feels diminished in the light of Mowgli's privilege: "Thou art of the Jungle and *not* of the Jungle," he reminds Mowgli, "and I am only a black panther" (p. 165). In spite of his aloofness, Mowgli retains all the pleasures of fraternity: "He is blood-brother to every beast in der *rukh* [jungle]," avows Muller, the head forest ranger, with a touch of envy (p. 331).

Through his unique education, then, Mowgli becomes a fraternal despot, and bridges the gap that usually divides an alien ruler from his subjects. Or so Kipling asserts. But is the resolution Kipling proposes possible? Can the pleasures of fraternity, for instance, and those of absolute authority be enjoyed simultaneously in a single set of relationships? A close look at the theme of brotherhood in *The Jungle Book* shows that such a fusion is impossible, and points up the moral tawdriness of Kipling's dream as well.

The incompatibility of fraternal and despotic bonds becomes most obvious when Kipling recklessly juxtaposes them; angry at Bagheera, the panther, "Mowgli stared, as he had stared at the rebellious cubs, full in the beryl-green eyes till . . . the eyes dropped, and the big head with them—dropped lower and lower, and the red rasp of a tongue grated on Mowgli's instep. 'Brother—Brother—Brother!' the boy whispered" (pp. 164-165). When we imagine the scene, the fully grown panther abasing himself before the fierce-eyed child, it is impossible to reconcile the deed with the words, the enforced humiliation with the rhetoric of intimate equality. Brothers quarrel, and one brother may find himself subject to the authority of another, but the terms of brotherhood preclude arbitrary domination and humiliation. When Mowgli addresses the creature prostrated beneath his foot as "brother," he is bestowing a feudal favor, not proclaiming a felt bond of mutual respect and equality.

Yet the psychology of the scene is by no means improbable. The rhetoric of brotherhood serves to soften the harsh reality of absolute power both for Mowgli and for Bagheera. Mowgli gains from his declaration a partial release from the fear and loneliness of absolute rule; after all, it is uncomfortable to have a panther at your feet, even if he is only licking them. Bagheera, too, gains a release from anxiety, since the pledge of brotherhood implies a bond based on love rather than on power. But it is difficult to imagine such a fabric of shared deception providing either party with a true sense of security.

The immorality of Kipling's dream of fraternal despotism is evident in the ways in which Mowgli violates the bonds of brotherhood. Mowgli's eyes are his strongest weapons, and he uses them not only to stare the animals into submission, but also to extract their knowledge. What Mowgli does with his eyes reveals his true identity to be that of a spy, for while he uses them to take in the many secrets revealed in good faith by his jungle brothers, he keeps them closed to the animals' gaze. "The mouth is angry," observes Bagheera during another contest with Mowgli, "but the eyes say nothing. Hunting, eating, or swimming, it is all one—like a stone in wet or dry weather" (p. 262). The aloofness that Strickland achieves by disguise, and more conventional imperialists by clubs and compounds, Mowgli achieves through his eyes, which serve as one-way windows, concealing his knowledge and deepest feelings from his animal brethren while allowing him to observe their every move. Thus Mowgli's claim of brotherhood is itself only a disguise; the passage continues, "Mowgli looked at [Bagheera] lazily from under his long eyelashes, and, as usual, the panther's head dropped. Bagheera knew his master" (p. 262).

Besides being morally reprehensible—a perversion of an essential human bond—this kind of a deception can succeed only for a limited time. Kipling's presentation of his program in the form of a beast fable serves to disguise this fact, for, since the animals cannot hope to equal humans in power, their ongoing collusion in the false but reassuring brotherhood offered by Mowgli is understandable. But the beasts of fable are also human beings, and human beings have a capacity to learn and develop that animals lack. When viewed in human terms, the jungle folk's continuing and ready acquiescence in the roles assigned them by Mowgli is unconvincing. The posture of elder brotherhood was one frequently adopted by imperial agents, but the historical tendency of the societies they ruled has never been toward increased stability. On the contrary, Bagheera's human counterparts have tended to endure their subordinate station only until they had the power to deny the mystifying claims of fraternal mutuality imposed by their alien masters. It is not surprising, then, that the unrealistic and unethical foundations of Kipling's social vision become more obvious when it is embodied in a specifically imperial setting.

Several stories written in the nineties present the new model of education and rule in an Indian setting. A new hero emerges in these stories, the "country-born" imperialist, the European who is born in India and who is exposed to the Indian community in much the same way that Mowgli is exposed to the community of the jungle. Kipling's country-born characters, of whom Kim is the best known, manifest a self-confident spirit that makes them far more attractive than the beleaguered, anxious protagonists of the earlier fiction. But they manifest, too, a conviction of their own superiority that is anything but attractive and that threatens to shatter the vast system of imperial government. They are the fictional forebears, in other words, of those European colonialists in countries like Rhodesia and Algeria who rebelled against their superiors in the imperial government, and did so in the name of Empire.

The first story in which to be country-born confers a special status is "The Son of His Father," published in 1893. The story opens with the announcement that Strickland and his wife have produced a child, Adam, who is "the first of men" in his small world.[4] Almost at once, the scene shifts to the camp of Strickland's Indian policemen, where the boy's birth is being discussed. The policemen's comments range over two central issues, the education the boy will receive and the condition of the Empire he will inherit. The men agree that country-born Englishmen make the strongest rulers, but disagree as to the future of the British Raj. A Naik tribesman whose wife is Adam's wet nurse argues that the English are losing control; by the time Adam is a man, he insists, "there will be no English in the land. . . . They are asking permission of clerks and low-caste men to continue their rule even now" (p.

279). Thus the stage is set for a crucial test: a new imperial man, an Adam, is emerging at a time of crisis.

Why do the country-born make the best rulers? The Indian policemen believe that children like Adam, suckled by Indian woman as Mowgli was by the wolves, "become blood of our own blood" (p. 278) and gain "double wisdom." This makes them both more sympathetic to their subjects and better rulers: "When he is a Police officer," one Indian says of Adam, "it will be very bad for the thieves" (p. 279). There are other immediate advantages as well, for the country-born child grows up in a climate of security and deference in which the instinct to rule develops naturally and not as a compensation for a sense of fear and impotence, an expression of pent-up hostility. Adam as a child enjoys on a microcosmic level the very essence of the imperial dream: "But, as his legs grew under him, he found that by scaling an enormous rampart—three feet of broken-down mud wall at the end of the garden—he could come into a ready-made kingdom where every one was his slave" (p. 282). Unlike his English-born fellows, the country-born child begins to act the imperial ruler from the moment he learns to walk. Within the kingdom of the police compound Adam, like Mowgli in the jungle, is both child and father. The police form "a ring of kind faces and strong arms" (p. 283) to protect him from evil, but they also bow "to the dust before him" (p. 277) in deference to his racial authority.

Adam's education, then, closely resembles Mowgli's. The basic qualities instilled by their experiences are self-confidence and cultural amphibiousness. Both take it for granted that they are innately superior to the citizens of the community they rule, and yet both feel completely at home in that community. Adam's name, like Mowgli's, testifies to his amphibiousness. The Indian policemen mistake his name for an Indian one: "They will call him Adam, and no jaw-splitting English name. Ud-daam" (p. 280). Like Mowgli the Frog, Adam-Ud-daam will be at home in two worlds.

The positive implications of Adam's education for the future of British rule are made clear early in the story. One day Adam's nurse is inadvertently present when the boy receives an unjust punishment from his father. Mortified at what he considers an insult to his honor, and humiliated that an Indian woman should have witnessed it, Adam demands that the Naik's wife be dismissed. When Strickland reluctantly agrees, the child himself gives the order:

> "Imam Din, tell thy Naik that his woman is dismissed from my service."
> "Huzoor!" said Imam Din, stooping low.
> "For no fault of hers."
> "Protector of the Poor!" (p. 288)

Thus the Naik's assertion that the English no longer have the spirit to rule is tested and disproved. Adam asks permission of no one; when he is angered he issues orders that command obedience. The Naik, we may assume, learns not to underestimate his masters, and the reader learns that a country-born European makes a better autocrat.

But Kipling is acutely aware that such an upbringing as Adam's may threaten imperial rule even while it seems to reinforce it. The major conflict in "The Son of His Father" is not between Adam and the Indians, but between Adam and his father. What Kipling realizes, finally, is that children educated in superiority make unwilling servants. The rise of the country-born poses a threat to the power of the father and thus to that of the fatherland.

The two worlds of Adam's childhood are analogous to the two realms of Empire. Within the walls of the family compound, Adam is a subordinate member of the dominant community. He enjoys many privileges, but ultimately he must defer to his father and submit to his judgments. In this sense, Adam's position in the family resembles that of the imperial officer in the government he serves. On the other side of the wall, however, things are different. Among the Indians, Adam is a king.

Conflict arises because Adam takes his sense of identity increasingly from his role in the Indian community. When Strickland punishes him severely, the child rebels and carries out a plan of revenge that makes a fool of his father. He refuses, in other words, to recognize his father's authority, the authority of England. "I am little, and you are big," Adam proclaims. "If I stayed among my horse folk I should not have been whipped. *You* are afraid to go there" (p. 286). Adam's revolt epitomizes that of imperial field officers and colonialists, who, as they grew increasingly confident in their own strength and increasingly independent of England, also grew more and more reluctant to accept discipline and directions from above. If the experience of childhood in the Indian community aggravates this tendency, it may have the ironic effect of perfecting the imperialist's ability to rule and, at the same time, destroying the Empire of which he is a part.

Kipling's response to this threat in "The Son of His Father" is ambivalent. Strickland, clearly still a respected voice, admires his son's confidence, cunning, and knowledge. Irritated by the stupidity of an English-born subordinate, he even argues for a degree of separation: " 'Now that's just what I want that young fool not to do,' said Strickland. 'He hasn't passed the lower standard yet, and he's an English boy born and bred, and his father before him. He has about as much tact as a bull, and he won't work quietly under my Inspector. I wish the Government would keep our service for country-born men. Those first five or six years give a man a pull that lasts him his life' " (p. 301). But Strickland also fears his son's independence and willfulness. Adam's rebellion produces an immediate reaction in his parents: "Strickland took long counsel with his wife, and she with the cheque-book and their lean bank-account, and they decided that Adam must go 'home' to his aunts" (pp. 291–292). "Home" is where Strickland himself was sent to have his colonial ways "flicked . . . out . . . with a wet towel at Harrow" (p. 284). The father is sending his son back to England to be broken.

But where does Kipling stand? Does he ratify Strickland's decision? Although the story provides no definitive answer, it suggests that Kipling's attitude toward the traditional program is one of increasing resistance. Strickland himself does not enjoy the prospect of sending his son away. As for the Indians, they approve of Adam's behavior, and consider his concept of honor appropriate to his station. Finally, Kipling clearly enjoys the child's rebellion and revenge and thus, implicitly at least, underwrites the larger struggle for

autonomy from English dominance and discipline. Not until *Kim,*
however, will he openly advocate the abolition of exile to England.

Kipling's identification of the country-born imperialist as a new
breed and his tentative approval of a country-born rebellion against
imperial authority combine fantasy with fact. His vision of a second
generation of less neurotic imperial rulers anticipates and is cor-
roborated by a leading social psychologist of imperialism, O. Mannoni, who observed it in action in colonial Madagascar. Mannoni's
first-generation imperialist, like Kipling's, feels a deep sense of inadequacy and a compensatory need to dominate others. And Mannoni, like Kipling, argues that a new type of imperialist emerges in
the second generation:

> A distinction must be drawn between those Europeans who were
> born and brought up in a colony—they are still in the minority, at
> least among adults—and those who were born and bred in Europe
> . . . Europeans born in a colony are unlike their parents. They do
> not as a rule suffer from an over-compensated inferiority complex,
> as do the parents . . . In a colonial environment the fact of belong-
> ing to the privileged race offers easy compensations for inferiority
> and certainly diminishes its effects, and the children usually possess
> very firm and un-neurotic racial convictions . . . Such convictions
> are obviously based on the childhood experience of seeing the father
> exercise absolute authority over all Malagasies—an authority which
> to the child is unquestioned and unquestionable. Later these
> children begin to feel superior even to metropolitan Europeans . . .
> because they are absolutely convinced, without any neurotic com-
> plication, of their superiority to the natives, while the Europeans
> have not that complete assurance.[5]

Mannoni's country-born French imperialists are virtually identical
to Kipling's country-born Anglo-Indians; Kipling's dream of a new
imperial man is clearly not entirely a wish-fulfilling fantasy.

Kipling even seems to be aware of a potential flaw in the personality of the country-born imperialist. Mannoni, who sees inferiority as the "main driving force of Western man . . . which sets
him apart from all other peoples in the world," makes a great deal
of this flaw. Without the impetus of inferiority, he argues, the
country-born are likely to be "far less worthy products than are

Europeans."[6] Kipling seems to be expressing a similar fear indirectly at one point in "The Son of His Father." When one policeman wonders why the English send their children home, another replies, "To give them that devil's restlessness which endures for all their lives. Whence we of Hind have trouble" (p. 278). The ironic possibility implicit in both Mannoni's and Kipling's statements is that it may take a painful sense of inferiority to generate the energy needed to enforce imperial despotism. If this is so, then tormenting self-doubt is a necessary ingredient in the successful despot's personality, and Kipling's desire to eliminate this "flaw" from the imperial mold is dangerous folly. Kipling never again explores this possibility; instead, he continues to suggest that the country-born imperialist will be the better ruler, and he eventually comes to oppose any exposure of future imperial servants to the inferiority-producing climate of European society.

What neither Kipling nor Mannoni seems to recognize fully is the fragility of that idyllic environment in which their country-born imperialists grow up. Only so long as imperial authority remained absolute and unquestionable were country-born children untroubled by intimations of inferiority. As soon as this authority was questioned, as soon as the imperial rulers were forced into a defensive posture, the atmosphere of colonial childhood became tainted with fear and anxiety. And the challenge to authority was inevitable, for the imperialists brought with them new tools and ideas that they could not keep forever from the colonized peoples. The African writer Ezekiel Mphahlele eloquently describes the process by which the atmosphere of insecurity was reintroduced in South Africa:

> I thought of those early days in a bush school when one began to recognize the written word in a reader. The words leapt like fire in front of one, seemed to splutter and send off sparks to illuminate so much of the world depicted in the reader. In the upper classes one became aware of much more, and even life in a squalid urban ghetto generated its own energy, which destroyed some and hurled others onto the steel gates of white privilege. And when the white man heard the gates shake, he knew he was never going to enjoy a quiet sleep.[7]

While Adam Strickland was climbing over the mud wall of his family compound into the ready-made kingdom where everyone was his slave, Indians of the National Congress movement, men educated like Mphahlele, were already knocking at the front gate of Anglo-Indian privilege. Soon the walls of the British compounds were reinforced, and excursions like Adam's became impossible. Kipling, too, soon had to abandon his excursions into fantasies of ready-made rule, but in the nineties he chose to dream on while the forces of a new reality gathered at the gates.

Kim is Kipling's richest dream. The "great and beautiful" India it depicts with a spirit of celebration dazzles the reader, especially if he comes to it across the bitter landscape of the earlier stories. In those, India is a grim realm of exile; in *Kim,* it is the very heart of life. Responding to this spirit in *Kim,* Mark Kinkead-Weekes offers the book as "the answer to nine-tenths of the charges levelled against Kipling and the refutation of most of the generalisations about him."[8]

This does not seem to me to be the case. Rather, I believe *Kim* represents at best only a partial victory for Kipling over the authoritarian elements in his own personality, a victory achieved not by grappling with these elements but by retiring into a fantasy world where they can exist side by side with finer ideals of fraternity and tolerance. Once again in *Kim,* though in a far more subtle fashion than in *The Jungle Book,* brotherhood and despotism keep uneasy company. Although Kipling finds a way to reconcile the Empire's need for bureaucratic chains of command with the imperialist's dream of autonomy, his method, that of making *Kim* a spy, raises important ethical and political questions.

The generous spirit animating *Kim* has been widely praised by Kipling's admirers. J. M. S. Tompkins, for instance, is pleased to note that "the sympathies of the book are inclusive not exclusive," and Kinkead-Weekes also finds in *Kim* a welcome change of spirit: "The eye is caught by a whole kaleidoscope of race, caste, custom, and creed, all seen with a warm affection that is almost unique in Kipling."[9] How Kipling, so long an advocate of caste distinctions and feudal hierarchies, achieves this atmosphere of affectionate inclusiveness reveals both *Kim*'s virtues and its weaknesses.

The structure of *Kim* contributes much to the impression of inclusiveness. Picaresque in its organization, the narrative follows
Kim in his travels across India. Kim, himself of course, provides the
thread of continuity, tying together the many distinct episodes just
as he does the disparate worlds they illuminate. But cohesion is
basically taken for granted; the stress is on the variegated beauty of
what is included. India lies before Kim and the reader like the plat-
ter of jewels in Lugran Sahib's shop. This larger structural casual-
ness is reflected in the many vivid catalogues Kipling presents in
Kim.

The action of the book encompasses much of India, moving the
reader from west to east along the Grand Trunk Road, and from
the sweltering south to the superb Himalayan north. In both directions the roads reveal the plentitude of life. On the road north to
Simla,

> it was all pure delight—the wandering road, climbing, dipping, and
> sweeping about the growing spurs; the flush of the morning laid
> along the distant snows; the branched cacti; tier upon tier on the
> stony hillsides; the voices of a thousand water-channels; the chatter
> of the monkeys; the solemn deodars, climbing one after another
> with down-drooped branches; the vista of the Plains rolled out far
> beneath them; the incessant twanging of the tonga-horns and the
> wild rush of the led-horses when a tonga swung round a curve.[10]

While the glories of the northern road are primarily natural, those
of the Grand Trunk Road are exuberantly human: " 'All castes and
kinds of men move here. Look! Brahmins and chumars, bankers
and tinkers, barbers and bunnyas, pilgrims and potters—all the
world going and coming . . .' And truly the Grand Trunk Road is
a wonderful spectacle. It runs straight, bearing without crowding
India's traffic for fifteen hundred miles—such a river of life as
nowhere else exits in the world" (p. 94). As the book continues,
the metaphor of the road as river merges with the other great
metaphor of inclusion, that of the lama's Wheel of Life on which all
men are bound in their "thousand thousand shapes." The lama seeks
to escape from road and wheel alike, but Kim finds both
fascinating: "by the roadside trundled the very Wheel itself, eating,
drinking, trading, marrying, and quarrelling—all warmly alive"

(pp. 346–347). Kim's ambition, which he achieves, is to live at the very center of the wheel, in the heart of life.

Another image of inclusion in *Kim* is the family. Like Mowgli and Adam, Kim is freed from the exclusive bonds of his real family to become the "Little Friend of all the World" and "son" to "Half Hind." Lionel Trilling considers this expansion of the family to be one of the book's chief delights: "*Kim* . . . is full of wonderful fathers, all dedicated men in their different ways, each representing a different possibility of existence, and the charm of each is the greater because the boy need not commit himself to one alone."[11] Almost all of us have grown up in some version of the nuclear family, surrounded by an indifferent society, stunted, perhaps, by the smallness of our intimate world. We have all been forced, as we have matured, to make exclusive choices. Thus in terms of our own society as well as that of the Indian Empire, Kim's privilege is enormous.

Finally, from the perspective of this study, the most significant inclusion in *Kim* is that of the alien imperialist in the culture he rules. Kim's upbringing, so unconventional and so similar to that of Mowgli and Adam, is the vehicle of this transformation; Kim emerges from childhood as both son and father of a vast Indian family.

The plot of *Kim* parallels those of *The Jungle Book* and, to a lesser extent, of "The Son of His Father." Like the heroes of these works, and unlike most Anglo-Indian children, Kim is exiled not to an English world of hostile authority, but to the ready-made kingdom of India. The loss of his parents, which cuts him off from the exclusive world of the imperial community, saves him from the exile and oppression that would ordinarily have been his lot, and catapults him into the very heart of his homeland, India. Like Mowgli and Adam, Kim enters this exotic world as a privileged member of the superior race. Like them, he is soon surrounded by a protective ring of fathers—Ali, the lama, Colonel Creighton, and others—who protect and educate him. With their support, Kim grows ever wiser, freer, and more confident. At last he is ready to assume a place among the imperial elite of the secret service. In assuming this role, moreover, he transforms it, for he brings to it a set of skills and sympathies not heretofore available in a white man. Like Mowgli and Adam, he is the first of a new breed.

In *Kim*, however, Kipling resolves the question left unsettled in "The Son of His Father." The notion of the country-born hero first introduced in the earlier story now undergoes a final logical metamorphosis, and what emerges is the idea of the "country-born and bred" hero who grows up entirely in India. Kim has the ultimate in country breedings, but the youths he meets at St. Xavier's School are also country-bred, and he approves of their ways: "Kim watched, listened, and approved. This was not insipid, single-word talk of [English] drummer-boys. It dealt with a life he knew and in part understood. The atmosphere suited him" (p. 204). The stories Kim hears reveal that the country-born possess a fearless familiarity with India:

> There were boys of fifteen who had spent a day and a half on an islet in the middle of a flooded river, taking charge, as by right, of a camp of frantic pilgrims returning from a shrine; there were seniors who had requisitioned a chance-met Rajah's elephant, in the name of St. Francis Xavier, when the rains once blotted out the cart-track that led to their father's estate, and had all but lost the huge beast in a quicksand. There was a boy who, he said, and none doubted, had helped his father to beat off with rifles from the verandah a rush of Akas in the days when those head-hunters were bold against lonely plantations. (p. 203)

Assumed superiority, eagerness for command, and familiarity with India are the common denominators of these anecdotes; Kim's schoolmates, like Adam Strickland, never ask permission of Indians.

Kipling wants us to approve of these boys, and to recognize their superiority to English-born-and-bred imperialists. These are the men, Kipling insists, who should be ruling India. As the Sahiba, Kim's adopted mother, puts it, "These be the sort to oversee justice. They know the land and the customs of the land. The others, all new from Europe, suckled by white women and learning our tongues from books, are worse than the pestilence. They do harm to Kings" (p. 125). *Kim* is replete with such criticisms of the English-born imperial official, the "genuine imported Sahib from England" (p. 248). Soldiers and administrators alike are ridiculed for their "dull fat eyes," their blindness to India. Kim's young tormentor during his brief stay with the Irish regiment is the type of all such imperialists: "He did not care for any of the bazars which were in bounds. He styled all natives 'niggers'; yet servants and sweepers called him abominable names to his face, and, misled by their deferential attitude, he never understood" (p. 174). Ignorance insures isolation; the same drummer-boy tells Kim all the English soldiers agree that "in this bloomin' Injia you're only a prisoner at large" (p. 168). Kim, forced to wear a uniform, finds that it "crippled body and mind alike" and when he travels second class, like an Englishman, he is lonely and longs for the pleasure of company in third class. The English-born-and-bred, Kipling suggests, live desiccated lives in the very midst of India's living stream.

In *Kim,* then, the inclusion of the imperialist is made contingent on his being country-born-and-bred. Kipling had distrusted certain English liberal notions of imperial rule for years. He had, along with the Orientalist group in the Indian Civil Service, resented the intrusion of English Members of Parliament and high civil servants in local affairs. And he had hated his memories of persecution in an English home and school. The calamities of the Boer War, in progress while he was writing *Kim,* probably helped convince him finally that the colonies should avoid contamination from England. But *Kim* does not explore the exclusive and separatist implications of the celebration of the country-born. Instead, Kipling focuses on the country-born imperialist's inclusion in the society he rules. It is Kim's membership in this society that is kept constantly before our eyes.

The last chapters of *Kim* are filled with gestures of inclusion that affirm Kim's status as a privileged member of the Indian family. Perhaps the most dramatic of these is Kim's symbolic union with the Woman of Shamlegh. After the struggle with the Russian spies, Kim and the lama retire to the mountain village of Shamlegh. The head of this village is an impressive Indian woman whose fondness for Kim leads her first to try to seduce him and then, when she realizes that he is bound to save the ailing lama, to give him valuable assistance.

This episode does not reveal its full significance unless the reader recognizes the Woman of Shamlegh as Lispeth, the heroine of the early Kipling story of the same name. The Woman's history, which she relates to Kim, recapitulates the plot of the earlier story: " 'Once, long ago, if thou canst believe, a Sahib looked on me with favour. Once, long ago, I wore European clothes at the Mission-house yonder.' She pointed towards Kotgarh. 'Once, long ago, I was *Ker-lis-ti-an* and spoke English—as the Sahibs speak it. Yes. My Sahib said he would return and wed me—yes, wed me. He went away—I had nursed him when he was sick—but he never returned.' " (p. 431). Here is "Lispeth of the Kotgarh Mission," the heroine of the Kipling story most critical of imperial rule, reappearing after fourteen years.

Kipling reintroduces her at this time, I believe, in order to impress on us the superiority of country-bred rulers. Lispeth's pain, Kipling suggests in the earlier story, stems from the ignorance and aloofness of the English. Her lover does not recognize her as a fellow human being, nor does he accept the obligations such a recognition would entail. Instead, he takes her love and deludes her as to his own feelings, while all the time planning his return to England and to his English fiancée. His careless betrayal of a marriage pledge suggests the larger betrayal of the Indian people by their English rulers.

Kipling has Kim meet Lispeth to show that such betrayals are not inevitable. Kim's situation resembles that of the earlier European: he is aided and wooed by Lispeth in much the same way. But whereas the earlier figure, repaying kindness with deception, makes pledges he does not plan to keep, Kim deals with the Woman of Shamlegh frankly, fairly, and generously. She wants him as a lover, and he apparently refuses her, but he does reveal his true identity in an embrace and a kiss, for which she blesses him. And when she gives him money, he is careful to see it restored to her.

The full significance of their relationship emerges in the echoes

set off by her last question, "you will come back again?" (p. 435).
These words, recalling the faithlessness of her first lover, suggest
the difference between him and Kim. He was English-born, and
had his heart set on a return to England. Kim, however, is deeply
bound to India; he wants nothing more than to continue exploring
its many roads. In a sense, he is already wed to the country, committed by his upbringing and his vocation to a life as a benevolent
ruler of her people. His kiss seals this commitment, and symbolizes
not only his inclusion but also that of his fellow country-born-and-
bred Englishmen within the culture they are to rule.

For someone who has read through Kipling's Indian works, this
episode is particularly moving and unexpected. It suggests that all
along, as Kipling is praising his imperial heroes, depicting their sac-
rifices, exploring the weaknesses that make India hell for them, he
is also thinking of how they fail their subjects, and looking for ways
to mend this flaw as well as the others. Reference to the imperial
breach of faith reemerges, perhaps for political reasons, only when
Kipling has what he considers a solution to the problem, a mold
that will form the ideal benevolent despot. Then, in an act of
breathtaking inclusiveness, he reintroduces Lispeth and invites us to
read *Kim* not alone, but in the context of all his Indian works—a
history that ends in the achievement of social harmony.

Once again, however, there is a darker side to Kipling's gesture
of inclusion. For if Kim will not desert the Indian peoples, neither
will he leave their land and thus liberate them. The faithless Englishman of the early story at least does not impose himself on India
for eternity; he has a home to go to. The country-born-and-bred
Anglo-Indian, on the other hand, considers India his home. Kipling, praised by Tompkins for so generously including the Indians
within the world he portrays with sympathy, is actually busy trying
to make a permanent place for people like himself at the top of their
social hierarchy.

In other ways as well, the spirit of inclusiveness in *Kim* is neither
so ethically sound nor so universal as it may first appear. Kim's own
commitment to inclusiveness lacks depth, and the inclusive spirit of
the book is predicated on a primary exclusion of considerable mag-

nitude. The exclusive tendencies in Kim's own personality emerge in his relation with Colonel Creighton of the espionage service. Kim, the "Friend of all the World" (p. 222) takes immediately to Creighton as "a man after his own heart—a tortuous and indirect person playing a hidden game" (p. 191). In Creighton's presence he becomes a "queer, silent, self-possesed boy" (p. 209). Kim himself, then, is by no means entirely loving and inclusive. The model of human relations implicit in Creighton's personality and profession would, if universalized, render community, friendship, and openness shams and establish policy and power as the sole determinants of human contact. Yet when Kim is forced to choose between his loving relation with the lama and his contract with Creighton, he puts the contract and all it implies first. He employs the lama as a screen in his engagement with the Russian spies, deflecting the old man from his spiritual search and putting his life in jeopardy. The lama continues to love Kim after this incident, and Kim shows great affection for him. But the fact remains that Kim, in choosing to manipulate the old man, expose him to danger, and use him as an instrument, has made an important personal choice for cold exclusiveness. This choice is further confirmed at the book's end, when Kim decides to continue his work as a spy.

Another kind of exclusion provides the basis for the inclusive atmosphere of *Kim* as a whole. For the book's inclusiveness is achieved not through a vision that successfully reconciles the contradictions at work in imperial India, but through primary acts of exclusion that annihilate the troubling aspects of the Indian situation, preserving only those elements of Indian life of which Kipling approves.

On the most accessible level, certain affects are clearly excluded from the emotional climate of *Kim*, as several critics have noticed. Kinkead-Weekes, for instance, observes that "Kim's junior version of 'the Great Game'—his stealthy commissions on the housetops—involves danger, intrigue, and worldly knowledge of a sort, but it hardly supports the claim that 'he had known all evil since he could speak.' Indeed, the world is strangely disinfected as it passes through Kim's eyes."[12] Kipling dramatizes elsewhere what it is like for a child to know all evil—that is the theme of "Baa Baa, Black Sheep"—but Kim certainly endures no such crushing experience. If he knows all evil, he knows it in a very different way from Punch, a way that, as Kinkead-Weekes suggests with a metaphor from medicine, inoculates both him and the reader against its poison.

Herein lies the key to another form of exclusiveness in *Kim*. The consciousness of the main character, in fact the very existence of that character, is not human at all, but divine in the manner of the pagan gods of mythology, who walked the earth enjoying human pleasures but free from human travail. Kim never encounters evil and pain in the same terrible, immediate way as the imperialists of the earlier stories. And since the reader is invited to identify with Kim, he, too, experiences India from this godlike vantage point. Having precluded the possibility of pain and evil, Kipling can easily create the impression of joyous all-inclusiveness.

Because Kim is a god, India is a kind of paradise. It has its dangers, but only enough to keep things interesting. For the rest, the country Kipling called a house of torment and compared with hell is described now as a "great good-tempered world" (p. 57), a "great and beautiful land" (p. 222), and "the kindly East" (p. 346). Part of this transformation is legitimate, for Kipling's theme is that to a country-born-and-bred European India is a familiar home, not a foreign prison. But much of the transformation involves a gigantic act of imaginative disinfection. Kipling simply wipes out, erases from his picture of India, all those groups and forces that were making life there in his time difficult for any imperialist, country-born or not.

The two social forces that most infuriated Kipling and his fellow imperial officials are nowhere to be found in *Kim*. These forces, the imperial administrative hierarchy and the emerging nationalist Indian bourgeoisie, appear frequently in the early stories as objects of exasperation and anger. But now the administrative hierarchy figures only tangentially, in a few references to its obtuseness, and the only Western-educated Indian is a gifted spy and aspiring member of the Royal Society.

In place of the bureaucratic hierarchy, the weight of which crushes many Kipling heroes in the stories of the eighties, there is in

Kim the wonderful, mysterious abstraction called the Game, an espionage network "so large that one sees but a little at a time" (p. 277). The players follow orders, but share a common love of their dangerous vocation. Moreover, the very secrecy of their work confers a certain freedom, for between them and the visible government there can be little contact. "Cannot the Government protect?" asks Kim of a fellow agent. "We of the Game are beyond protection" is the reply (p. 328). But by the same token they are to a considerable extent beyond control.

And yet to treat the Game, as Kipling does, as if it were some utterly autonomous activity, with its own laws and life, is to distort reality. Here is another version of Kipling's old dream of autonomous despotism and licensed anarchy, only this time the confining geographical boundaries are down, and the middle-level imperial officer ranges over an entire Empire. In fact, however, the imperial bureaucracy remained, sending down assignments, defining larger goals, and undoubtedly checking, however fitfully, too independent subordinates. And the other team is rarely defeated quite so easily in life as Kim defeats them in Kipling's fiction. We know enough of the work of spies to realize that Kipling and the many popular writers since who make the world of espionage the last realm of heroic individualism are merely dreaming.

Finally, Kipling excludes from *Kim* not only the imperial antagonists of the official in the field but also his Indian enemies. In order to paint a picture of a harmonious India reconciled to imperial rule Kipling has no alternative but to exclude the Indian nationalists entirely, and he does so. Huree Chunder Mookerjee, the only Western-educated Indian in *Kim*, betrays no nationalistic sentiments whatsoever. Nor, as several critics have pointed out, are any of the efforts of the Game directed against the nationalists. Indeed, all of Kim's enemies come from beyond the border of British India. Within these borders, all is amity. Such was not the case, of course, nor is there any reason to conclude that Kipling's basic attitudes have changed when, after writing numerous stories that criticize the nationalists bitterly, he writes a book celebrating an India from which they are completely missing. In fact, *Kim* achieves its inclu-

sive spirit by an imaginative annihilation of Kipling's perpetual enemies.

What Kipling excludes, ultimately, is history, the vital forces
changing Indian society. He does so by focusing on either side of
the historical process, on the plentitude of the moment and the
finality of the eternal. The highways and bazaars are the locus of
Kim's world of the moment; the great patterns of the Game and the
Search provide the eternal frame. Both realms are finally static, for a
vision of the moment may record motion, but it can hardly discover
the dynamics of that motion, the direction of change. And from the
vantage point of the eternal ("When every one is dead the Great
Game is finished. Not before" [p. 362]), change loses much of its
significance. Only by means of this exclusion can Kipling evade the
truth that the British position in India is deteriorating rather than
improving.

Only at one point, and then perhaps unconsciously, does Kipling
suggest the fragility of the world he celebrates in *Kim*. This is when
he writes of the ancient lama's passion for the mountains he is leaving forever: "He blessed them in detail—the great glaciers, the
naked rocks, the piled moraines and tumbled shale; dry upland, hidden salt-lake, age-old timber and fruitful water-shot valley one after
the other, as a dying man blesses his folk" (p. 422). The lama's style
of prayer is Kipling's style of writing in *Kim*. The book, with its
many catalogues of wonders, is a blessing in detail of a dream of India, a dream held by many men besides Kipling. Yet in this case it is
not the suppliant but the dream that is dying, and in this sense *Kim*
is as much an elegy as a prescription for change.

What the discovery of all these exclusions leads to, finally, is the
recognition that the generous inclusiveness of *Kim* is in the spirit of
wish fulfillment, not of hard-won victory or compromise. Kipling
has surrendered nothing; his "kindly East" is a land that accepts as
its natural rulers the very group to which he himself belongs—the
country-born Englishman. Nor has he resolved the contradictions
in the imperial system that crippled the imperialist's personality and
frustrated his longings for absolute, unchallenged authority. The
India of *Kim* is a world from which Kipling's enemies, and those of

his fellow imperialists, have been magically banished. Who could not write generously about such a world? But we need not be surprised when in years to come, as the Empire begins to disintegrate, Kipling turns once again to polemic and invective, displaying the same authoritarian traits rendered largely invisible in *Kim*.

In his efforts to eliminate the flaws in the imperial mold, Kipling devises an educational program that depends on social inequality for its success and aims at making inequality permanent. Kim, Mowgli, Adam Strickland, and the thousands of country-born colonial children they represent achieve their invulnerability artificially, like the sons of feudal lords, by virtue of their race. Their childhood exercise of authority over adults of the subject community convinces' them of their inherent superiority and of the naturalness of continued despotic rule. They grow, in other words, neither into submissive adults nor into cooperative ones but into the fundamentally dominating type of authoritarian described by Mannoni as one product of imperialism.

But the bastions of racial privilege were already under attack when Kipling began to write, and the social system on which his new model depended was already slipping into the past. Thus Kipling arrives, at the turn of the century and the peak of his career, at the archetypal condition of the European colonialist as seen by Mannoni. He is a man projecting fantasies of omnipotence onto a world that bears less and less resemblance to his dream. This is at once a pathetic situation and a dangerous one, for while Kipling did his projecting with a pen, the men he idolized and encouraged more often used the sword. To see Kipling's situation more clearly, we need only turn to Conrad, who portrays the dreaming colonialist brilliantly in figures like Tom Lingard, Lord Jim, and Kurtz.

4

JOSEPH CONRAD:
BOUND TO EMPIRE

The psychology of individuals, even in the most extreme instances,
reflects the general effect of the fears and hopes of its time.
CONRAD, "Autocracy and War"

Although his youth was spent in Eastern Europe and at sea, Joseph Conrad, like Rudyard Kipling, grew up in the realm of imperial forces. In Poland and around the world, he saw the effects of imperialism. And in his own personality and the personalities of people close to him he recognized the psychological roots of empire. Through these many experiences, Conrad developed the vision of imperialism expressed in his fiction. By looking briefly at his life, therefore, it is possible to see how that vision grew, what shape it took, and why, in spite of some similarities, it is antithetical to Kipling's.

As Raskin has pointed out, Joseph Conrad grew up a native in a colonized country.[1] From the moment of his birth, Józef Teodor Konrad Korzeniowski was molded by the forces of imperial struggle. The Ukraine, where he was born in 1857, was part of the Polish kingdom for four hundred years. Then in 1793, in the second of three partitions that cost Poland her autonomy, the Ukraine was turned over to imperial Russia. A series of unsuccessful rebellions ensued; at Conrad's birth, yet another was only six years in the future.

Conrad's parents, Apollo and Ewa Korzeniowski, belonged to

the faction of the Polish nationalist movement that sought not only independence from Russia but also land reform and the abolition of serfdom. They paid heavily for their commitment. In 1861, Apollo, whose once wealthy family had lost almost all its property as a result of its participation in earlier rebellions, organized a clandestine revolutionary committee in Warsaw. Arrested by the police for this and other activities, he was imprisoned for seven months. Then he and Ewa were tried before a military tribunal and sentenced to exile in a remote part of Russia. Conrad, only four, accompanied his parents into exile.

For all of them the next years were ones of protracted sickness and suffering. Conrad almost died of pneumonia on the long journey to Vologda. His mother also grew ill almost immediately, and never completely recovered. The circle of misery widened in 1863, when word reached the exiles of the defeat of the rebellion they had helped to plan, and of the deaths of many friends and relatives. Then in 1865 Conrad's mother died of tuberculosis. Her death was a terrible blow to father and son alike. Apollo tried to provide for his son's emotional and material needs, but his own health and spirit were disintegrating under the blows of exile, bereavement, and disease. For four more years he struggled along, trying to insure Conrad a safe future; allowed to return to Poland in 1868, he died in Cracow in 1869. Conrad was an orphan at the age of eleven.

Apollo Korzeniowski's sickness and death brought his son to the brink of madness. In "Poland Revisited" Conrad recalls the long hours of hopeless waiting; had it not been for the escape of reading, he writes, "I would have had nothing to do but sit and watch the awful stillness of the sick room flow out through the closed door and coldly enfold my scared heart. I suppose that in a futile childish way I would have gone crazy."[2] As it was, when Conrad took his place at the head of the massive funeral procession organized by the people of Cracow for his father, he was, according to his grandmother, in "utter, inconsolable despair."[3]

Dr. Bernard Meyer, in his psychoanalytic biography of Conrad, asserts that Ewa Korzeniowski's death "engendered within [Conrad] a sense of having been abandoned. For however well a small child may seem to accept a rational explanation of illness and death, such explanations usually fail to obliterate the feeling of having been rejected."[4] Apollo Korzeniowski's death compounded the problem, Meyer believes, and left Conrad with a very weak sense of identity and with intense feelings of insecurity and inadequacy. As he grew up, he struggled to overcome these feelings through identification with strong men and with positions of command. At the same time, however, he sought the shelter of subordination as a refuge from self-doubt. (Meyer uses this theory to help explain Conrad's uneven career as a master mariner.) A similar pattern, Meyer argues, is observable in Conrad's friendships; these "tended . . . to take the form of protector and protégé, with Conrad occupying now one role and now the other, rather than to assume a pattern of a mutual exchange between two co-equal adults."[5]

Thus Conrad, like Kipling, grew up in exile and lost his parents at an early age. But their experiences were by no means identical. While Kipling was exposed from the age of five to the unmediated hostility of strangers, Conrad's parents and guardians sheltered him as much as possible from the violence of society. At first this task fell mainly to his mother, but after her death his father took it up. Writing from exile, Apollo Korzeniowski reports of Joseph, "I shield him from the atmosphere of this place, and he grows up as though in a monastic cell."[6] Nor did his father's death thrust Conrad into a hostile world; Ewa's family, the Bobrowskis, whom Conrad had known for years, took him in immediately and cared for him until he went to sea. Tadeusz Bobrowski, his mother's brother, gave him both love and advice, so that Conrad in later years considered him a second father.[7]

Thus although Conrad's childhood left terrible scars, they did not include those produced by direct exposure to violence, cruelty, and oppression. Conrad, unlike Kipling, did not have to develop a pattern of deception and ruthless aggression to deal with his immediate environment. Nor did he have to suppress tremendous fears and hatreds, storing them up to be released later in the form of aggression. It was not necessary for him to avoid introspection and expression; his family shared their feelings instead of burying them. Conrad may have developed the doubts and desires that dispose men toward authoritarianism, but not the self-blindness and rage. The absence of these qualities made his life no easier, but it allowed him a depth and breadth of vision such as Kipling never achieved.

A further distinction exists between Conrad's early experience of suffering and Kipling's. Although both suffered because of imperialism, Kipling's sufferings were interpreted to him by his parents and society as necessary to the preservation of security and justice in a larger community, whereas Conrad's were interpeted to him as the result of an unjust and unnatural state of affairs. Kipling was invited to place the ultimate responsibility for his suffering on humanity's innate depravity and the need to control foreign savages. Conrad was invited to blame his sufferings largely on the aggressive intrusion of a foreign state into a coherent community. Kipling was educated to believe that imperialism ultimately reduced suffering; Conrad, to believe that it needlessly augmented it.

But Conrad's family itself was not entirely free from imperial attitudes and allegiances. Apollo Korzeniowski sacrificed himself to the dream of national liberation, but he sacrificed his family as well. He contributed to his wife's death and abandoned his son, all in the name of that dream. Was his act selfless or sublimely egotistical? Did he owe primary allegiance to the dream or to his family? Conrad was deeply troubled by these questions, which were kept before his mind by Tadeusz Bobrowski, who blamed Apollo for the death of his sister. Meyer argues that Conrad's criticisms of the imperial father figures in his fiction are in fact based on his perception of his own father: "The picture of the fictional father as a self-centered man whose single-minded dedication to a fixed idea is responsible for widespread misery and even disaster must represent one facet, at least, of Conrad's judgment of Apollo Korzeniowski."[8]

Although Meyer's identification of Conrad's real and fictional fathers is convincing, figures like Tom Lingard and Jim are by no means simply fictionalized projections of Apollo Korzeniowski. The personalities of Conrad's imperial father figures resemble not only Apollo's personality but also that of the typical colonialist as Mannoni describes him. Both Apollo and Mannoni's colonialist are egotistical men who impose private visions of reality on the people whose lives they control, with disastrous effects. It may be more likely, then, that Conrad, bitterly aware of these traits in his father, recognized them again when he came in contact with men like Lingard and Jim, and drew a realistic picture of these figures in his fiction. The importance of the connection between Conrad's real and fictional fathers, in my opinion, is that it helps to explain Conrad's insights into, fascination with, and distrust of the imperial figures he so accurately describes.

Avrom Fleishman, in *Conrad's Politics*, calls attention to yet another way in which Conrad's family was involved in imperial problems. Instead of stressing Conrad's childhood experience as a colonized native, Fleishman makes the point that the Korzeniowskis were themselves a family of colonialists. He achieves this shift in perspective by focusing his attention on facts other scholars have relegated to footnotes. Conrad's father, he observes, came from Podolia, a region that had belonged to Poland for four hundred years before the Russian occupation, but in which only 12 percent of the population were ethnic Poles. This minority, descendants of colonizers, owned most of the land. A similar situation, Fleishman goes on to point out, prevailed in the province of the Ukraine, where Conrad spent his first four years on an estate managed by his father, and where the Bobrowskis had their property. In the Ukraine Poles made up only 3 percent of the population, but once again they owned most of the land.[9]

Fleishman believes that both Conrad's personality and his ideas were shaped by his colonial heritage. As the son of colonialists, Fleishman suggests, Conrad probably experienced "an insidious sense of alienation in early childhood, a sense of living among strangers, surrounded by darkness." And the colonialist heritage, he argues, determined some of Conrad's "more subtle feelings about imperialism," leading him to distinguish between conquerers and colonialists in his evaluation of imperialism: "In the final analysis [for Conrad] colonization is a viable—the only viable—form of imperialism."[10] Characters like Lingard and Jim, Fleishman contends, reflect Conrad's approval of the colonialist.

Conrad does seem to have felt a stronger sympathy for established colonial elites than for the agents of late nineteenth-century imperialism. But in the Malay novels, at least, the established settlers are not Europeans like Lingard and Jim, but people of the Malayan archipelago itself. In the archipelago of Conrad's day, as in the Ukraine, three parties were competing for power: various indigenous peoples, more or less closely related groups of warrior-rulers, and the Europeans. Of these three, the group that most closely corresponds to Conrad's own in the Ukraine is not the Europeans but the warrior-rulers, who are threatened both by the Europeans and by the people they have been accustomed to rule. And it is to this group—to figures like Hassim in *The Rescue* and Dain Waris in *Lord Jim*—that Conrad gives his most undivided sympathy. If the European protagonists of these tales are to be identified with any of the parties in the Ukrainian dispute, it must be with the hated Russians. I do not believe, then, that Conrad's own colonial heritage led him to identify uncritically with modern European imperialists.

In 1874, at the age of sixteen, Conrad left Poland to go to sea. Poland, with its memories of vain struggle, death, and despair, its promise only of harassment, and its threat of conscription into the Russian army, offered little to the young man. But by becoming a sailor, Conrad did not leave behind him the imperial conflicts that had blasted his childhood. His two decades in the merchant marine took him, at the outset of the last great surge of imperial expansion, into all the major arenas of conquest: into Latin America in 1875 and 1876, the Far East from 1883 until 1888, and Africa in 1890. During these years, when empire became an obsession throughout Europe, Conrad sailed back and forth between the great commercial centers and tiny "outposts of progress." And

everywhere, up rivers in Borneo and the Congo, at forgotten settlements in the Caribbean, and around hotel tables in numerous imperial cities, he exchanged goods and tales with scores of imperial
adventurers.

Jocelyn Baines, John Gordan, Norman Sherry, and other scholars
have shown how strong a presence these men and places are in Conrad's fiction.[11] They have demonstrated conclusively that Conrad
found the models for his fictional Tom Lingard, Almayer, Lord
Jim, and Kurtz in men he either knew or knew about in the colonial world: in William and Jim Lingard, William Olmeijer, Arthur
Hodister, and Georges Klein. Rajah James Brooke, an Englishman
famous as the ruler of an eastern kingdom, also fired Conrad's imagination.

Sherry in particular has shown that Conrad's use of these models
extended beyond superficialities. Conrad, Sherry shows, observed
and dramatized their personalities as well as their exploits. The real
William Lingard, for instance, seems to have shared his fictional
brother's egotism, his desire for power and acclaim. He seems, too,
to have shared Captain Tom Lingard's habit of adopting protégés.
And he took pride in his unofficial title of "Rajah Laut," or "King
of the Sea."[12] Thus the psychology of Conrad's imperial fiction, like
the settings, is historically authentic. Conrad was as serious an
observer of colonial psychology as Mannoni was later to be, and he
anticipated many of Mannoni's insights.

Conrad's opportunities to examine the psychological
dynamics of imperialism did not end even when he gave up
the sea to become writer, or so he implies when he calls attention to
the similarities between the writer's explorations and orderings and
those of the imperialist. In his discussions of these similarities, he
moves from a sympathetic to a critical treatment of the imperialist,
from an identification of the two vocations to a careful discrimina-
tion in favor of the writer.

The comparison in the 1899 manuscript of "The Rescuer" is by far the most sympathetic in terms of Conrad's treatment of the imperialist. In it, the imperialist is described as "one of those unknown guides of civilization, who on the advancing edge of progress are administrators, warriors, creators . . . They are like great artists a mystery to the masses, appreciated only by the uninfluential few, wilfully neglected by the great who love ease. Their work lives, but the simple wisdom which has given the very quality of life to their work is hidden forever to the common mind."[13] Perhaps Conrad realized he had been caught up in the rhetoric of empire or carried away by enthusiasm for his analogy, for he omitted this passage from the published version of "The Rescuer" and never portrayed such a farsighted, heroic imperial warrior in his novels. But he did continue to find similarities between the artist and the imperialist.

His later observations reveal a certain disillusionment with both professions. While he was working on *Heart of Darkness,* for instance, Conrad complained in a letter to a friend of the atmosphere of unreality that surrounds the writer. He would soon, he promised, "come out of my land of mist peopled by shadows," back into the real world.[14] The land to which Conrad alludes is most obviously that of his imagination, but anyone who has read *Heart of Darkness* will recognize its similarity both to the upper reaches of Conrad's Congo and to the mental state of his imperialist characters. For both Marlow and Kurtz the Africans are shadows; to the former they are mysteries; to the latter, all too faithful servants of his most destructive dreams. Implicit in Conrad's statement, then, is the suggestion that artist and imperialist alike live in a world without others, a world where dream and reality can hardly be distinguished.

Once again in *A Personal Record* Conrad implicitly compares the artist and the imperialist. In this case, he is describing the artist's situation in the world of his imagination: "In that interior world where his thought and his emotions go seeking for the experience of imagined adventures, there are no policemen, no law, no pressure of circumstance or dread of opinion to keep him within bounds. Who then is going to say Nay to his temptations if not his conscience?"[15] In this clear echo of the famous passage in *Heart of*

Darkness ("solitude—utter solitude without a policeman—. . . silence—utter silence, where no warning voice of a kind neighbour can be heard whispering of public opinion"),[16] Conrad suggests that both the artist and the imperialist explore worlds in which there are no external controls over their deepest drives.

But he is quick to draw an essential moral distinction: "I think that all ambitions are lawful except those which climb upwards on the miseries or credulities of mankind. All intellectual and artistic ambitions are permissible, up to and even beyond the limit of prudent sanity. They can hurt no one."[17] With this statement Conrad strongly distinguishes between the imperialist's vocation and his own. The imperialist's adventures bring suffering to the peoples he encounters; his surrender to insanity threatens entire societies. The artist, on the other hand, can harm only himself in the course of such explorations. In drawing this distinction, Conrad may underestimate the artist's power, but he is certainly correct in insisting that the artist's conquests are different in quality from the imperialist's.

Alan Sandison's argument that Conrad's cognitive idea and the imperial idea were identical breaks down before this distinction. Sandison states that Conrad's need to secure his own identity "dictated an incessant war against an alien and chaotic nature with the elusive end in the subjugation of the latter. This crisis, where the principal is at once aggressive and embattled in a foreign and menacing world which he nevertheless seeks to appropriate, is essentially the crisis of empire. The embarkation of the self on its rapacious cognitive conquest to overcome the world's 'otherness' thus finds an equivalent physical expression in the imperial idea."[18] Implicit in this argument is the conclusion that Conrad, by approving of one activity, also approved of the other. But Conrad distinguished correctly between his intellectual adventures and such political adventures as those of the imperialist and he denied the morality of the latter. Precisely because he works with his own memories, perceptions, and impulses and not with the lives of other people, the artist is innocent of immoral aggression and conquest. He may share some of the imperialist's drives, and even some of the dangers he runs, but he does not participate in the imperialist's appropriation of other people's lives and lands. Thus although Conrad uses his experience as an artist to help himself understand the imperialist, only once—in a passage later discarded—does he apologize for imperialism by calling its heroes artists.

 Throughout his life, then, Conrad was learning about imperialism, and his continuous immersion in imperial issues made his choice of imperial settings and conflicts almost inevitable. The artist draws on experience, especially on the experience of conflict. The locus of the great and even of the many minor conflicts to which Conrad was exposed as a child and young man was imperial. The powers of empire determined the fate of his family and homeland; the winds of imperial trade blew him around the world; and the atmosphere of imperial strife pervaded the cities and settlements wherever he landed. No wonder, then, that he chose colonial settings for most of his works, imperial issues for the political themes of his novels, and imperial personalities as the subjects of some of his finest psychological analyses. What is extraordinary is that so many critics have ignored or denied both the influence of imperialism on his life and its place as a central problem in his work.

Its influence both on the life and on the work was profound. In the realm of psychology, Conrad's experiences provided him with deep insights into the imperial personality; his understanding of his own and his father's personalities helped him understand the imperial figures he later met. Like Marlow, he recognized in these men qualities similar to his own, and, like Marlow, he pursued resemblances only to arrive at a clear sense of differences. The typical imperialist was egocentric, needed to be in charge, and tended to impose a private vision of reality on the world around him. But the imperialist also acted blindly, without any sense of his own fallibility or of the rights of others. He lacked restraint, and in the colonies the normal social constraints were missing.

Conrad's recognition of these differences in personality provided him with the plots and character configurations of *Heart of Darkness* and *Lord Jim*, in which Kurtz and Marlow and Jim and Marlow meet to illuminate the complex fatality that attends the egotistical dreamer. The same recognition also provided him with an explanation of the imperialist's moral failure, one that challenged the popular argument that the colonizer was corrupted by the people he conquered. In Conrad's fiction the colonizer does not "revert to savagery" or "go native" in the sense of taking on the traits of the people he conquers. His fall is the product of his own desires and the license he gains by being white, owning weapons, and living beyond the borders of his own community.

Indeed, Conrad's whole perspective on imperialism differed fundamentally from that of other English authors of his time and provided him with a uniquely broad view of the issues. Alone among writers like Kipling, Haggard, Henley, and Stevenson, Conrad lived both as a native of a colonized country and as a member of a colonizing community. Thus he achieved what they never could, although some, like Kipling, tried: a view from the other side of the compound wall. Having stood among the colonized, he could never accept the most basic issues of empire as resolved. As a result, while Kipling writes mostly about the conflicts involved in perfecting the techniques of imperial domination, Conrad's works explore the issue of domination itself. He sees the imperial world, in other words, in terms of its most basic contradictions. And because he does, he claims for his subject a set of struggles far more central and complex than those on which Kipling focuses.

In many ways, then, Conrad's experience provided him with the knowledge needed to challenge imperialism. At the same time, however, the succession of traumas he endured and the number of successful imperial incursions he witnessed instilled in him a pessimism that robbed his criticism of considerable power. As a child he knew the loneliness and uncertainty of exile and the pain of abandonment. As a young man, he saw social patterns like those that had been the source of his own misery being laid down over most of the world. The impact of his early experience, then, was intensified by his observation of similar suffering on a vast scale. Nor was there much cause, in Conrad's experience, for hope that the process might be checked and reversed. In the flawed but powerful solidarity of his family, in the traditions of the agrarian squirearchy to which it belonged, and in those of the merchant marine Conrad saw what he considered to be a more humane order. But he had seen his family shattered and his class submerged under the tides of autocratic expansion. And the community of the merchant marine seemed threatened by the advent of steam and the emergence of class conflict. Bound as he was by experience of and sympathy with these models of community, Conrad had his best hopes demolished by their proven fragility. Unlike Kipling, he could in no way identify with the new masters. Nor could he agree with the terms of their servants' rebellion. Thus he came to adopt that position of principled despair so common in this century. And he suffered terrible bouts of depression, its inevitable psychological corollary.

But Conrad also waged a constant battle against the temptation to universalize the suffering and moral chaos of his age. He refused to embrace fully the implications of his pessimistic vision. He could not resign himself to the inevitability of empires, or to their triumph. He could not surrender humanity to an eternity of folly and cruelty. He was conscious of his own inconsistency, and refers to it in a letter to the Scottish writer and radical Cunninghame Graham. The subject is the Spanish-American War, and Conrad writes, "I am sorry, horribly sorry [for Spain]. *Au diable! Après tout cela doit m'être absolument égal.* But it isn't, for some obscure reason or other. Which shows my folly."[19] Although he goes on in this letter to vilify the human race and declare his indifference to its fate, Conrad clearly isn't indifferent, and his commitment to a vision of a more humane society is evident in the very bitterness of his attack.

Conrad's work, too, makes clear both his inclination and his deep antipathy to such universal pessimism. Although he focuses frequently on human blindness and cruelty, he almost always maintains an engagement with concrete historical events, the abandonment of which signals the modern writer's surrender to political despair. This engagement may be in part negative—a method of proving the case against humanity with the best evidence available; but it is also, I believe, a function of Conrad's moral vision and larger hopes. By insisting on the significance of temporal, spatial, and cultural boundaries he holds out hope that the world he describes is not the only world, not inevitable. In his treatment of character, as well, Conrad resists the idea that the current chaos is eternally ordained. The flexibility of social conditions and of the human personality, he suggests, renders all situations contingent. Thus, although Conrad resembles other modern writers in his deep sense of human irrationality and social chaos, he differs from many of them in his stubborn commitment to a historical vision and a standard of values.

One of Conrad's aims, in his fiction, is to convey the complexity of experience, the elusiveness of truth. His treatment of imperialism reflects this aim. He offers descriptions, explanations, and evaluations of imperialism, but does so provisionally, without achieving either absolute consistency or certainty. Thus any attempt to synthesize Conrad's vision of imperialism involves drawing some conclusions, taking some risks. I do not mean to suggest, however, that no synthesis is possible—only that it is bound to be both speculative and somewhat controversial.

Of Conrad's fundamental opposition to imperialism there can be no doubt. As he portrays it, imperialism is basically an expansion of capitalist or autocratic drives beyond national boundaries. The nature of these drives is aggressive and exploitative, and their effect is to destroy what is most human in people and their communities. Furthermore, the dynamics of these drives are to a large extent self-perpetuating; their very destruction of values and traditions creates the conditions for even more aggressiveness and exploitation. Capitalism destroys the values and traditions of the old European states. Under its pressures all relationships are reduced to a matter of wealth and power. The vast majority of people are humiliated and exploited; they find themselves producing "variegated rubbish

. . . for the benefit of a few employers."[20] Under these conditions fear and greed flourish as everyone becomes more anxious for security, which seems to lie only in the accumulation of wealth and the achievement of domination. Sympathies atrophy while dreams of power take on added urgency. The powerful, insecure even in their power, appropriate all the tokens of strength and dignity they can, thus exploiting the rest of the people psychologically as well as economically.

Eventually the pressures of competition drive more and more people abroad. These exiles satisfy their needs for wealth and superiority by conquering and exploiting communities around the world. They destroy these communities as Europe itself has been destroyed, and leave the peoples they encounter in a similar state of cultural anarchy. But in the empire, the European adventurer also meets his nemesis. The very thoroughness of his success is his downfall. The more his impulses are exercised, the stronger they become. The more his fantasies are fed, the more they grow until they entirely obscure his view. In the end he is unable to adjust either his needs or his self-image to the demands of reality. He leaves behind him, however, a world in social, moral, and psychological decline.

Conrad developed this view of imperialism not only from first-hand experience but through much reflection as well. It is consonant with his larger vision of human beings and society, a vision rooted in the ideas of his class and time. As Fleishman has so well demonstrated, Conrad belongs to the tradition of organic conservatism identified in England with Edmund Burke. The assumptions of that tradition are implicit in his attitude towards imperialism. Conrad's commitment to the Burkean idea of the organic community sets him at odds with capitalism and imperialism. Like Burke and his followers, Conrad rejects the optimistic individualism of Adam Smith and Rousseau. Neither the marketplace nor the wildwood, he insists, nurtures humanity properly; the individual becomes human only in the context of a closely knit organic community. In the hostile loneliness of the market and the forest, he can only act the beast.

But such communities, based on shared experience, values, and traditions and offering liberty without license, cannot be legislated into existence. They must grow with time. Thus when capitalism and imperialism intrude, destroying the structures of community, they are doing terrible damage to real human hopes in the name of an illusory dream. The idea of cultural pluralism implicit in the notion of organic communities further reinforces Conrad's hostility to imperialism. The organic metaphor suggests that each community will develop at its own pace and in its own direction. When the imperialist intervenes, therefore, with his rhetoric of civilization and his real gift of cultural anarchy and foreign rule, he is both intellectually misguided and practically destructive. Neither his rationalization nor his action is sound.

Yet his effect is devastating. Unlike Burke, Conrad sees little hope for the survival of organic communities. The process of destruction, viewed with alarm by the English conservative at the end of the eighteenth century, has gone too far to be reversed by the end of the nineteenth. Capitalism has proven too strong an acid: "*Il n'y a plus d'Europe*—there is only an armed and trading continent, the home of slowly maturing economical contests for life and death, and of loudly proclaimed world-wide ambitions."[21] Conrad makes this declaration in "Autocracy and War" (1905), the most extensive statement of his political beliefs. He goes on to sum up the pretense and the reality of those worldwide ambitions in a single bitter phrase; the capitalist nations are eager, he writes, "for the privilege of improving the nigger (as a buying machine)." With the entire human community reduced to "a House of Strife," Conrad finds himself a Burkean conservative in a Hobbesian world.[22]

Conrad's psychological beliefs, like his political ideas, are grounded in the conviction that the individual is deeply influenced by his society. Conrad's is, in other words, a social psychological perspective. But what are the terms of the relation between the individual and the community? At times Conrad suggests that people are inherently depraved, endowed with immutable destructive instincts. In this view of the human being as an "*animal méchant*"[23] and society as a form of protective custody, Conrad anticipates those psychologists who argue that human aggressiveness is biologically founded and can only be constrained, never significantly diminished.

On other occasions, however, Conrad suggests that human nature is not so immutably fixed, and that the influence of community for good or evil is considerable. In a letter to Graham, he writes, "Not that I think mankind intrinsically bad. It is only silly and cowardly. Now *you* know that in cowardice is every evil—especially, that cruelty so characteristic of our civilization."[24] In these words Conrad does not abandon the instinctualist position for the institutionalist, since he still assumes that men are endowed with certain basic instincts. But the instincts he attributes to humanity, silliness and cowardice, are far more general, more susceptible to mitigation, than is an innate instinct toward aggression. What is more, the connection he draws between fear and cruelty and the impression he gives that European civilization is particularly cruel suggest that the aggressiveness of the modern European is based on feelings of insecurity that have been greatly intensified by the conditions of capitalism. In another context as well, Conrad shows that he sees the problem of psychological aggression at least partly in social terms. "The spirit of aggressiveness," he claims in "The Crime of Partition" (1919), "was absolutely foreign to the Polish temperament, to which the preservation of its institutions and its liberties was much more precious than any ideas of conquest."[25] Implicit in this statement is the idea that certain societies encourage the spirit of aggressiveness and so predispose their members to imperial adventures.

Conrad's fictional insights into the psychological dynamics of imperialism have a fullness and intensity that could only have come from immediate experience. He had gotten in the way of empire; he had felt its power. And it had gotten into him, into his father; he had known its urgency. Through everything, by some miracle of courage and genius, he had brought to bear on his experiences a critical and speculative intelligence. But it is in the works themselves that the power of his insights is most apparent.

5

THE MALAY NOVELS:
IMPERIAL ROMANCE AND REALITY

In the midst of these dark-faced men, his stalwart figure in white apparel, the gleaming clusters of his fair hair, seemed to catch all the sunshine that trickled through the cracks in the closed shutters of that dim hall, with its walls of mats and a roof of thatch. He appeared like a creature not only of another kind but of another essence.

CONRAD, *Lord Jim*

Joseph Conrad's fiction carries us into the realm of Rudyard Kipling's dreams, into lands where the net of imperial bureaucracy is not so tightly woven as in India, and where isolated Europeans still rule entire communities. This is the situation that Kipling celebrates with bitter nostalgia, the situation of the lone district officer surrounded by his adoring subjects; it is the Victorian dream of the Middle Ages recreated in India only to be destroyed by the increasingly centralized administration of English-born, utilitarian civil servants.

Conrad, like Kipling, was fascinated by these isolated European rulers, by their personal destinies and the destinies of the peoples they ruled, and wrote some of his finest novels about them. In his work, as in Kipling's, a certain picture develops and a certain judgment, more or less implicit, is made. In Kipling's fiction, these Europeans rediscover in India the joys of life in an earlier time, the age of medieval chivalry so celebrated by Victorian poets and essayists. As rulers of the subject peoples, they enjoy a lordly and heroic status that sets them above their decadent European kin. In

Conrad's fiction, on the other hand, isolated European rulers act in a manner that ultimately destroys them and that illuminates the immorality of European expansion. The colonial lord emerges not as an exception to the deterioration of European civilization but as the epitome of that deterioration, the carrier of the disease.

In order to recognize the rhetorical element in Conrad's portrayal of imperial life, it is useful to understand the terms of the debate that was raging as he wrote. I do not mean to imply that Conrad's purpose was primarily polemical, but it must have been obvious to him, writing on imperialism at the turn of the century, that even to describe an imperial scene, even to focus on a single obscure and fictionalized colonial ruler, was to participate in a debate on the nature and motivation of expansion in which the opposing sides shared almost no common ground.

Conrad's works speak directly to two major questions in the imperial debate: the question of motivation and that of impact. Were Europeans assuming the "white man's burden"[1] to save themselves and their savage kin? Or were they thronging to the darker continents on missions of economic and psychological exploitation? Were they bestowing "civilization" on savages, or, as a small minority of critics argued, destroying cultures less powerful but in some respects more sound than their own? On both these major questions Conrad opposes the imperialists. His Malay novels—*Almayer's Folly, An Outcast of the Islands, The Rescue,* and *Lord Jim*—present a complex, socially grounded, and highly critical portrait of the colonialist's motives and mode of conduct.

In the Author's Note to *Almayer's Folly* (1895), Conrad attacks the stereotypic European view of non-European cultures. Many Europeans, he observes, have the impression that in "distant lands all joy is a yell and a war dance, all pathos is a howl and a ghastly grin of filed teeth, and that the solution of all problems is found in the barrel of a revolver or on the point of an assegai." They are wrong, he insists, and yet their error is understandable, for although "the picture of life, there as here, is drawn with the same elaboration of detail, coloured with the same tints . . . in the cruel serenity of the sky, under the merciless brilliance of the sun, the dazzled eye misses the delicate detail, sees only the strong outlines, while the colours, in the steady light, seem crude and without shadow. Nevertheless it is the same picture."[2] Conrad's argument, with its emphasis on lighting, draws on the theories of impressionism to describe the phenomena of ethnocentricity and racism. There may be an element of literal truth in his explanation, but its main thrust is metaphorical; he calls attention to the fact that any outsider will find it difficult to *see* with clarity the significant customs and values of the group he encounters. We are all "dazzled" by strangeness, and we are likely to find the experience threatening.

Having notified the reader that the stereotypic views of alien peoples are false, Conrad proceeds to make a statement that in his time must have been both shocking and offensive. There are no basic differences, he contends, between Europeans and "that humanity so far away": "I am content to sympathize with common mortals, no matter where they live; in houses or in tents, in the streets under a fog, or in the forests behind the dark line of dismal mangroves that fringe the vast solitude of the sea" (p. x). Implicit in Conrad's statement is the assumption that his eyes are adjusted to the glare of the tropics and that he sees its peoples clearly. Implicit, too, and this is most significant, is the suggestion that his art, by embodying his more authentic vision, will destroy the stereotypes prevalent in Europe and help create a sense of human solidarity. This, I believe, is the often disguised social project of Conrad's serious colonial fiction, a project that he himself could neither justify nor—for many years—abandon, and one that many of his scholarly admirers have overlooked. They have preferred to interpret him instead in terms of the deeply pessimistic formulation of the final lines of the Preface to *The Nigger of the "Narcissus,"* where Conrad writes of capturing, not the true picture of alien cultures, but a "surrounding vision of form and colour" and where he dedicates himself not to developing his audience's view of mankind, but to eliciting "a look . . . a sigh . . . a smile."[3]

The Author's Note sends us into *Almayer's Folly* with two questions in mind. If the stereotypic view of "native" peoples is wrong, what are they really like, and in what specific ways is the picture of their life identical to that of the life of Europeans? Answers to these questions are not easy to come by, for *Almayer's Folly* is very much a first novel. Conrad's ability to render character is unsteady, and his narrator seems to interpret omniscience as a license for self-contradiction. Nevertheless, the novel does clarify and dramatize the arguments put forward in the Author's Note.

At first glance, both the characters and narrator seem to belie the assertions of the Author's Note altogether. Conrad talks of solidarity and common mortals, but his characters are either rogues and fools (Babalatchi and Almayer) or creatures out of romance (Nina Almayer and Dain Maroola). The former seem too despicable, the latter too implausible, to evoke feelings of solidarity. But all do possess qualities that might be seen as part of a common fund of human potentiality. We may recognize ourselves in Almayer's penchant for dreams, Babalatchi's craftiness, Nina's longing for dignity, Dain's passion. Conrad's vision of human unity encompasses both vice and virtue.

If it is difficult to find an affirmation of solidarity in Conrad's presentation of his characters, it is almost impossible to reconcile the narrator's voice with that of Conrad in the Author's Note. The narrator assumes a dichotomy between civilized and savage humanity and resorts frequently to the rhetoric of racism, as when he talks of the unrestrained "savage nature" of Dain Maroola, and of the "savage moods" that compel Mrs. Almayer to demolish the civilized furniture of her home. Even though characters such as Babalatchi and Dain Maroola are credited with eloquence, diplomatic tact, "great power," "determination," and "dignity," they are still referred to as savages. No Malay, no matter how sophisticated or noble he may be, can escape the pejorative title; it is, therefore, clearly a racial one.

Nowhere is the discrepancy between what the narrator sees and what he makes of it more obvious than in his treatment of Nina Almayer. Her voice alone in the novel echoes Conrad's in the

Author's Note, yet the omniscient narrator constantly disparages
her insights. Next to the narrator himself, Nina has the widest access to the two worlds of *Almayer's Folly*. Because her father is
white, she gains a tenuous entry into the world of European colonial society. Because her mother is Malay and her family home is in
the remote settlement of Sambir, she also knows something of the
non-European world. Tolerated in both communities, completely
at home in neither, she sees them clearly and passes judgment.

Her initial conclusion is that both are despicable, that they are
equally sordid:

> It seemed to Nina that there was no change and no difference.
> Whether they traded in brick godowns or on the muddy river
> bank; whether they reached after much or little; whether they made
> love under the shadows of the great trees or in the shadow of the
> cathedral on the Singapore promenade; whether they plotted for
> their own ends under the protection of laws and according to the
> rules of Christian conduct, or whether they sought the gratification
> of their desires with the savage cunning and the unrestrained
> fierceness of natures as innocent of culture as their own immense
> and gloomy forests, Nina saw only the same manifestations of love
> and hate and of sordid greed chasing the uncertain dollar in all its
> multifarious and vanishing shapes.   (p. 43)

In this description of Nina's thoughts the bitter joke only hinted at
in the Author's Note becomes clear: it is not only that the Malays
are far more civilized than they first appear to European eyes, but
that the Europeans themselves are far less so than they believe.
Nina, who is the product of both races, can perceive the common
denominators of love and hate and greed at work in both. She
prefers the Malays because they seem less blind to the presence of
these forces, less given to disguising them with "sleek hypocrisy
. . . polite disguises . . . virtuous pretences" (p. 43). By her definition, "savagery" becomes synonymous with "sincerity." From the
Author's Note we might expect Conrad to support Nina's conception of the situation, if not her despairing commitment to savagery,
but the narrator's comment is that Nina has "lost the power to
discriminate" (p. 43). Once again the omniscient voice speaks out

for the very kinds of distinction that Conrad elsewhere rejects as blind, and that the story shows to be fatuous. What is Conrad up to?

Perhaps Conrad deliberately makes his narrator obtuse; perhaps he intends the narrator himself to dramatize the blindness of Europeans in the colonies, to show the power of mere words to create false and perfidious distinctions even in the most privileged observer. If this is Conrad's intent, and it well may be, then in *Almayer's Folly* he illustrates a fact still in need of repetition: to expose a prejudiced person to the objects of his prejudice will not necessarily enlighten him, since his experience of these objects will be predetermined by the terms he has for them. In Adorno's words, "One cannot 'correct' stereotypy by experience; he has to reconstitute the capacity for *having* experiences."[4] The narrator who sees everything misjudges because he sees in terms of racial categories.

But the narrator of *Almayer's Folly* is hardly a person at all; his invisibility and his omniscience discourage us from seeing him as a character, and force us to take what he says as the author's final word. Thus if Conrad is attempting to combine omniscience and obtuseness, the effect seems to me aesthetically unsatisfactory. There is, of course, another possible explanation for the narrator's unenlightened views. Conrad himself may have been deeply ambivalent about the true terms of the relations between Europeans and Malays, between "civilized" and "primitive" peoples. He may have felt, on one level or another, that the Malays were different and inferior, that their greed and hatred were of a different order from those of Europeans, or that they were trapped permanently, as many anthropologists argued, at a lower stage in the history of human development. But this explanation seems highly unlikely. In the first place, Conrad has his narrator describe the societies of Singapore and Sambir in a way that confirms Nina's belief that Europeans and Malays there are equally endowed with vices and virtues.

Moreover, by his treatment of Dain Maroola, Conrad suggest that the Malays' traditional precolonial culture was superior in important respects to that of modern Western civilization. Before Nina meets Dain, her view of both European and Malay societies is dominated by a perception of egotism, hatred, and greed; but Dain demonstrates to her that traditional Malay society, unlike the colonial society that has replaced it almost everywhere, also cultivated generosity, love, and courage. A prince of a great family, Dain comes to Sambir seeking the gunpowder he needs to repel European intruders and courts Nina, not for money, as Almayer courted her mother, but because he loves her. In pursuing these honorable ends he displays "openhanded generosity" and reckless courage; he appears to Nina, then, as "the ideal Malay chief of her mother's tradition" (p. 64).

Significantly, there is no counterpart to Dain Maroola in the European society of *Almayer's Folly*. (Tom Lingard, though a man of courage, is acquisitive and rootless; in the end he disappears, "swallowed up" by Europe.) Thus Dain is pitted against Almayer himself in a grotesquely one-sided contest for Nina's heart. Almayer's folly is palpable from the opening moments of the novel:

"Kaspar! Makan!"
The well-known shrill voice startled Almayer from his dream of splendid future in to the unpleasant realities of the present hour. An unpleasant voice too. He had heard it for many years, and with every year he liked it less. No matter; there would be an end to all this soon.
He shuffled uneasily, but took no further notice of the call. Leaning with both his elbows on the balustrade of the verandah, he went on looking fixedly at the great river that flowed—indifferent and hurried—before his eyes. He liked to look at it about the time of sunset; perhaps because at that time the sinking sun would spread a glowing gold tinge on the waters of the Pantai, and Almayer's thoughts were often busy with gold; gold he had failed to secure; gold the others had secured—dishonestly, of course—or gold he meant to secure yet, through his own honest exertions, for himself and Nina. He absorbed himself in his dream of wealth and power . . . They would live in Europe, he and his daughter. They would be rich and respected. Nobody would think of her mixed blood in the presence of her great beauty and of his immense wealth . . . All this was nearly within his reach. Let only Dain return! (pp. 3–4)

In these extraordinary first sentences of a first novel, Conrad evokes the complex perversity of Almayer's mind. Startled out of one daydream, Almayer ignores the call of reality and deliberately submerges himself again in tawdry and unrealistic fantasies of wealth and power. He uses the river, as in the end he will use opium, as a stimulus to distraction and places the responsibility for success, as he always has, on the back of another. The moment is paradigmatic of his entire history.

It is paradigmatic as well of the class to which he belongs. He is the first of Conrad's flabby colonialists, a forerunner of figures like Kayerts and Carlier in "An Outpost of Progress" (1898), the pilgrims of *Heart of Darkness* (1902), and Cornelius in *Lord Jim* (1900), men who pursue shabby dreams of material wealth with enervated spirits. Almayer's dreams are all of gold, and he attributes to it the power to overcome even the racial prejudice he feels so deeply himself. His pursuit of wealth, like theirs, is fitful and flabby; lacking the strength to act by himself, he depends first on Hudig, the trader, then on Lingard, and finally on Dain Maroola.

Conrad traces Almayer's weaknesses to his membership in the very element of European society that Kipling considers the great source of heroes: the country-born-and-bred colonials. While Kipling concentrates on the invigorating influences of a colonial childhood, Conrad gives a convincing picture of its debilitating effects. In Almayer's Java home, "the father grumbled all day at the stupidity of native gardeners, and the mother from the depths of her long easy chair bewailed the lost glories of Amsterdam, where she had been brought up, and of her position as the daughter of a cigar dealer there" (p. 5). Raised by a father who is privileged to complain but need not toil, and by a mother who sits dreaming of illusory glories, Almayer grows up in a world where power and labor, dream and reality, seem utterly unrelated. "Feeble and traditionless" himself, he represents a community and a civilization debased by narrow individualism, an unrealistic sense of history, and sordid aspirations.

Almayer's weaknesses rebound on his own family; he treats his wife as a slave and loves his daughter more as a projection of himself than as a human being with feelings and dreams of her own. Nina accepts her lot until Dain arrives, but then, recognizing the possibility of a nobler life, she rebels. "You wanted me to dream your dreams," she tells Almayer, "to see your own visions—the visions of life amongst the white faces of those who cast me out from their midst in angry contempt. But while you spoke I listened to the voice of my own self; then this man came, and all was still; there was only the murmur of his love" (p. 179). Nina's accusation illuminates the twin contradictions in Almayer's professions of love: he has been too concerned with his own dreams to attend to hers, and his dreams, based as they are on his prejudices, actually exclude her. "You call [Dain] a savage!" Nina cries. "What do you call my mother, your wife?" (p. 179).

Nina criticizes not only the racism inherent in European society, but its materialism as well. "You were speaking of gold then," she reminds Almayer, "but our ears were filled with the song of our love" (p. 179). Almayer's dreams are those of his cash-nexus society; Dain's more human preoccupations make him and the culture he represents seem superior. Thus Nina, cast by Conrad in the role of judge, chooses Malay culture over European. Events confirm the wisdom of her decision; the last we hear of her is that she has just borne a child and that there is "great rejoicing" in Bali, her new home. We hear, too, that the islands are preparing to rise against the Europeans, whose position is precarious. As for Almayer, he confirms his servitude to fantasy by becoming an opium smoker.

By his treatment of Dain, Conrad challenges imperial ideology even more radically than the Author's Note suggests he will. The relative healthiness of Dain's traditional Malay character in contrast to the characters of colonized Malays suggests that the Europeans, far from improving the Malays, have corrupted them. Conrad raises this possibility more than once in the novel. Thus when Mrs. Almayer, reproaching her husband's Malaysian adversary, Babalatchi, reminds him that "men with arms by their side acted otherwise when I was young," Babalatchi responds, "And where are they, the men of your youth? . . . Killed by the Dutch" (p. 155). Babalatchi's meaning is clear: the heroic qualities once encouraged by Malay society became suddenly suicidal with the advent of the Europeans; the new situation demands deception, craft, and real or feigned submissiveness. In so acknowledging the influence of social forces on human character, Conrad implicitly rejects the racist theories of inherent differences and inferiority supported by many imperialists. He also rejects, of course, the imperialists' claims to be improving the colonized peoples.

In *Almayer's Folly*, then, the European colonialists are not the modern knights of a new feudalism, but the wanton destroyers of living feudal communities. They are identified, and rightly, not with the forces opposed to commercialism and bourgeois values, but as forces spreading these values throughout the world. Thus even though Conrad himself is enchanted with the past, he refuses to be mystified by those who would cloak the future in its rhetoric. *Almayer's Folly* initiates, in a manner that is sometimes confusing, sometimes, perhaps, confused, a task of demystification that continues through Conrad's finest colonial novels. It is a remarkable beginning.

Kipling and other late Victorian apologists for imperialism liked to portray the relationship between colonized and colonizer in terms of the family: the natives were children; their European masters, gentle fathers. *An Outcast of the Islands* (1896), Conrad's second novel, explodes this self-flattering image of the imperialist not by denying the analogy altogether, but by affirming it in a new fashion. The imperialist is indeed a father, but not a benign one. Like the tyrannical fathers of Victorian fiction, Conrad's colonial paternalists mask authoritarian drives with the rhetoric of benevolence.

An Outcast of the Islands is the story of two men, Peter Willems and Tom Lingard, and of their Malay "families." Both men see themselves, and invite others to see them, as benevolent masters interested in the well-being of their dependents. Willems takes pride in the prestige he has conferred on the De Souzas by marrying into their family, while Lingard congratulates himself for having protected the people of Sambir from the contaminating influences of

European civilization. Yet the motives of both men are anything but altruistic; both take their greatest pleasure in the exercise of absolute power and control. Lingard's rationalization, in particular, has a broader political significance; his desire to preserve the Malays' traditional ways establishes him in the party of Kipling, the Orientalists, and all those who argued that the colonized peoples must be protected forever from contamination by Western culture. Thus *An Outcast of the Islands* challenges both the pretense of benevolent paternalism and the paternalistic program of relegating the colonized to an eternal dependence, a perpetual childhood.

The first paragraphs, which describe Peter Willems's self-image and suggest the real personality that image masks, establish the psychological and social framework of the entire novel. Willems lives comfortably in Macassar with his half-caste wife and her family, the De Souzas. Although he scorns the De Souzas, Willems also relies on them for the confirmation of his self-image: "That family's admiration was the great luxury of his life. It rounded and completed his existence in a perpetual assurance of unquestionable superiority. He loved to breathe the coarse incense they offered before the shrine of the successful white man."[5] As so often in Kipling's fiction, we are present in a world where authoritarian and colonial fantasies merge, where the categories of dominance and submission take substance in terms of god and mortal, white man and man of color.

Conrad begins his description of Willems rather mildly, making his despotic manner seem more than cruel. But as he probes deeper into Willems's motives and strategies, his tone becomes passionate with contempt. Willems, he reveals, achieves his status of divinity by treating the De Souzas inhumanely:

> He was their providence; he kept them singing his praises in the midst of their laziness, of their dirt, of their immense and hopeless squalor: and he was greatly delighted. They wanted much, but he could give them all they wanted without ruining himself. In exchange he had their silent fear, their loquacious love, their noisy veneration. It is a fine thing to be a providence, and to be told so on every day of one's life. It gives one a feeling of enormously remote

superiority, and Willems revelled in it. He did not analyze the state of his mind, but probably his greatest delight lay in the unexpressed but intimate conviction that, should he close his hand, all those admiring human beings would starve. His munificence had demoralized them. An easy task . . . This was power. Willems loved it. (p. 4)

Avid for superiority, Willems is perfectly content to achieve his goal by debasing others, rather than by improving himself. In fact, this is the preferable alternative, for he conceives of power as the capacity to make others suffer, and of superiority itself as a personal exemption from common suffering. Significantly, the colonial situation makes the realization of these perverse relationships "an easy task."

This passage, with its profound satiric analysis of domestic tyranny, has a Dickensian flavor. But Conrad is concerned with more than domestic tyranny. While Willems gratifies his authoritarian desires in the little world of the family, his Conradian double, Tom Lingard, gratifies similar urges by establishing himself as "father" to an entire community of Malays.

At first Lingard, hearty, indulgent, straightforward, and simple on a grand scale, so dwarfs Willems that their affinities are obscured. Yet the two men are closely linked: Willems is Lingard's protégé, and the older man evinces a disappointing pride in his unscrupulous charge. Why should the simple-hearted sailor Lingard admire a man who is "hopelessly at variance with the spirit of the sea" and with the "honest simplicity" of the seaman's vocation? (p. 17) The first suggestion is that Lingard's virtues blind him to Willems's faults, but as the story unfolds another answer emerges: Lingard manifests most of these faults himself. The role he has created for himself at Sambir closely resembles that of Willems at Macassar; the most significant difference is one of scale.

Conrad's evocation of Lingard's situation conveys its seductiveness:

He looked proudly upon his work. With every passing year he loved more the land, the people, the muddy river that, if he could help it, would carry no other craft but the *Flash* on its unclean and friendly surface. As he slowly warped his vessel up-stream he would scan with knowing looks the riverside clearings, and pronounce solemn judgment upon the prospect of the season's rice-crop. He knew every settler on the banks between the sea and Sambir; he knew their wives, their children; he knew every individual of the multi-coloured groups that, standing on the flimsy platforms of tiny reed dwellings built over the water, waved their hands and shouted shrilly: "O! Kapal Layer! Hai!" . . . He loved it all.   (pp. 200–201)

Like Willems, Lingard is enthralled by the bright dream of divinity. He perceives himself not as a greedy trader but as a benign father, and sees his monopoly as a sacred dispensation to the people of Sambir, a means of protecting them from European influence. Lingard's self-image seems finer, less corrupted by a crude urge to domination, than Willems's; we feel tempted to affirm the vision of the loving, slightly aloof father and the gracious, carefree children that this passage presents. But Conrad will not let us; he makes it clear that the dream world Lingard has imagined and half achieved is simultaneously a world of nightmare, and that Lingard's motives are as corrupt as Willems's. Before the novel is over, we have heard Lingard boast that "I have them all in my pocket . . . My word is law—and I am the only trader" (p. 43). And before the novel is over Lingard's children have rebelled, making a mockery of this boast.

Lingard's motives and illusions resemble Willems's in several respects. Just as Willems's domestic role is "the great luxury of his life," so Lingard's "queer monopoly" at Sambir constitutes "the greater part of his happiness" (p. 202). Just as Willems assumes that he has made the De Souza family happy, so Lingard boasts with equal blindness of Sambir that "there's peace and happiness there" (p. 45). Both men can be heard, one at the billiard table, the other in hotel lounges throughout the Archipelago, proclaiming their generosity, wisdom, and success.

Like Willems, then, Lingard realizes certain psychological profits, as well as economic ones, from his enterprise at Sambir. What is more, his method of extracting these profits closely parallels Willems's. This damaging fact comes out during an altercation with his agent Almayer, who demands angrily, " 'How many times haven't I saved this settlement from starvation? Absolute starvation.

Only three months ago I distributed again a lot of rice on credit. There was nothing to eat in this infernal place. They came begging on their knees. There isn't a man in Sambir, big or little, who is not in debt to Lingard & Co. Not one. You ought to be satisfied. You always said that was the right policy for us . . . Ah! Captain Lingard, a policy like that should be backed by loaded rifles . . .' " "You had them!' exclaimed Lingard" (p. 171). Lingard's "right policy," with its techniques of threatened starvation, perpetual indebtedness, and the threat of force, differs not at all from Willems's; in both cases apparently altruistic gestures serve the dual function of enslaving those at whom they are directed and deceiving any observers. And the deception, as in Willems's case, goes even deeper: Lingard himself believes that his motives are pure, his actions laudable. The deceivers deceive even themselves.

But they do not deceive their victims, at least not permanently. Lingard's Malay dependents see through his mystifying claims to benevolence and brotherhood. They protest against his dream with words and deeds, and compel us to see Lingard not merely as an individual imperialist, but as a figure embodying representative imperial motives and employing typical strategies. The most outspoken critic of Europeans is Aissa, Omar's daughter and Willems's lover. The foundation of her hatred is laid when European sailors wipe out her father's band of pirates: "They dropped whistling fireballs into the creek where our praus took refuge, and where they dared not follow men who had arms in their hands" (p. 46). The fact that Lingard is the leader of the European forces in this annihilating attack reinforces the sense that his benevolence is underwritten with ruthlessness, and that he exists in the novel as the embodiment of the imperial presence in all its forms.

Aissa generalizes with bitter eloquence about this presence. In her eyes, the Europeans are the savages, and Europe itself is "a land of lies and of evil from which nothing but misfortune ever comes to us—who are not white" (p. 144). Aissa's claim, antithetical to Lingard's, certainly proves true in her own case. Lingard and his sailors leave her homeless, and Willems lies to her, isolates her from her father, and finally denounces her with revulsion, leaving her in a condition of utter loneliness that reflects the large social and historical dislocation of her people. Each time Aissa's words are repeated—and they are voiced on four occasions in the novel—they seem more appropriate as a description of the colonial situation.

Babalatchi, too, makes an eloquent criticism of European domination. In the dark hours after Omar's death he confronts Lingard openly, without the mask of deference he has worn so long in the presence of the powerful white man. The immediate provocation for his outburst comes from Lingard himself, who offers a threadbare imperial justification for his long opposition to Babalatchi's ambitions:

> "If I ever spoke to Patalolo [Sambir's titular ruler], like an elder brother, it was for your good—for the good of all," said Lingard with great earnestness.
>
> "This is a white man's talk," exclaimed Babalatchi with bitter exultation. "I know you. That is how you talk while you load your guns and sharpen your swords; and when you are ready, then to those who are weak you say: 'Obey me and be happy, or die!' You are strange, you white men. You think it is only your wisdom and your virtue and your happiness that are true." (p. 226)

Here is the speech which Kipling's colonized beasts and humans, victims of the rhetoric of fraternal despotism, are never allowed to utter. Babalatchi demolishes Lingard's fraternal pose in an instant, dismissing it as a smokescreen behind which the imperialist gathers strength for the assault that will establish him in the only role that can satisfy him, the role of absolute ruler.

Babalatchi accuses Lingard and his fellows not only of deception, but of blindness or self-deception as well. His speech, an eloquent definition and denunciation of ethnocentricity, suggests a final flaw in the European program of paternal despotism, in the dream of a feudal empire. What Babaltchi points out is the tremendous gap that separates culture from culture and that makes a mockery of European pretensions to enlightened rule. Not only are Lingard's actions in Sambir distorted by his love of power and domination; they are distorted, too, by the alienness of his most altruistic in-

clinations. As for his claim to be protecting Sambir from European
incursion, this, too, is only partly true, for in taking control of the
community himself he has introduced alien notions of justice and
progress. Thus even the most benign imperialist can never truly
perform the function (advocated by Kipling and others) of protecting the colonized peoples from change. Whether such a program is
advocated naively or with the ulterior purpose of protecting monop-
olies on psychological and economic exploitation, it is doomed to
failure.

Conrad's attitude towards ethnocentricity is further illuminated in
his description of Lingard's reaction to Aissa's passionate avowal of
her love for Willems: "Lingard, outwardly impassive, with his eyes
fixed on the house, experienced that feeling of condemnation, deep-
seated, persuasive, and masterful; that illogical impulse of disapproval
which is half disgust, half vague fear, and that wakes up in our hearts
in the presence of anything . . . that is not run into the mould of our
own conscience; the accursed feeling made up of disdain, of anger,
and of the sense of superior virtue that leaves us deaf, blind, contemptuous and stupid before anything which is not like ourselves" (pp.
253–254). In Conrad's mind ethnocentricity, although perverse, is so
deeply rooted in the human psyche as to be incapable of elimination.
Even with the best intentions, then, the imperialist is likely to act op-
pressively; Conrad's hopes, therefore, are for the reestablishment of
the distance between cultures that once made coexistence possible.

Aissa, who tries to bridge the distance with love, fails utterly; in
the end, "hate filled the world, filled the space between them — the
hate of race, the hate of hopeless diversity, the hate of blood; the
hate against the man born in the land of lies and of evil from which
nothing but misfortune comes to those who are not white" (p.
359). But Babalatchi, by his patient scheming and close study of
European psychology, does induce Willems to show Abdulla, a
powerful trader, how to reach Sambir, and Abdulla in turn
dislodges Lingard from his place at the heart of the community.
Lingard belittles the achievement, observing that Babalatchi has
merely traded one white power, himself, for another, the Dutch

rulers introduced by Abdulla. But Babalatchi's rejoinder confirms his wisdom: "The farther away is the master, the easier it is for the slave, Tuan! You were too near. Your voice rang in our ears always. Now it is not going to be so" (p. 226). The Dutch, far off in Batavia, will have less control—either for good or for ill—over the lives of their foreign subjects. This is the kind of victory that Conrad, a child of Russian-occupied Poland, could appreciate.

One important aspect of *An Outcast of the Islands,* then, is the exploration of the complex reality behind European claims to be ruling in the Empire as paternal despots over nations of children. Conrad shows that the imperialists' motives can be considered paternal only in the authoritarian sense of that role, that their methods are deception and coercion, and that their goals are often demoralization and permanent domination. He shows, too, that the colonized peoples are neither brutes nor babies, and that they are capable of love and hate, sacrifice and policy. For these reasons, and because the Europeans' temporary success envelops them in fantasies of omnipotence, their incursions seem doomed to failure. But in the short run these incursions are the cause of great suffering, and in the long run whatever benefits they provide may be counterbalanced by the destruction of traditional values and customs.

The most powerful strategy Conrad employs to make these points is his juxtaposition of Willems and Lingard. By making Willems so blatantly authoritarian, Lingard so apparently benevolent, and then by revealing their basic similarities, he is able to dramatize the disjunction between imperial pretense and reality, and to explore the rationalizations by which imperialists convinced others and themselves of the rectitude of their project. A similar technique and similar themes animate *Heart of Darkness,* where the basic juxtaposition is condensed and temporalized in the history of Kurtz. But in *An Outcast of the Islands* the complex relation between Lingard and Willems is overshadowed by that between Willems and Aissa. The drama of disclosure is obscured as Conrad becomes entangled in what Thomas Moser calls his "uncongenial subject, romantic love."[6] As a result the novel, for all its insights, does not fulfill its potential.

"Religion and politics—always politics!" muses Edith Travers in *The Rescue* (1920) as she looks out over the Malay community, which Tom Lingard has mobilized for war.[7] "Always romance," the reader is tempted to rejoin, for Mrs. Travers's infatuating presence is about to cause the final collapse of Lingard's imperial dream, his plan to restore his Malay "brother" Hassim to power among the Wajo. In fact, political and romantic considerations often seem to be fundamentally at odds in *The Rescue*, so that one of the novel's conflicts might be defined in those terms. And when Lingard abandons his Malay allies for Edith Travers, romance may seem to be triumphant. But a closer look at the novel shows that Lingard surrenders to pressures that are sociopolitical as well as sexual. Son of a fisherman, Lingard flees England's class-bound society as a young man and redefines himself as a king in the colonies, where his inherent capabilities and his heritage (as a white) are not at odds. Then the Traverses, representatives of the English ruling class, invade his new world and automatically assign him to a subordinate role. Fatally distracted and demoralized, he allows his Malay friends to be destroyed while he devotes himself to his English masters.

Fleishman has this to say about the terms of the conflict and its resolution: "Lingard feels an inherited complex of ties to the Europeans, even before the added bond of his love for Mrs. Travers, and these prove stronger than his obligations to the natives. His choice shows the source of the inevitable failure of European intervention in native affairs."[8] Fleishman might have added that it also shows the hollowness of the imperial rhetoric of family, the constant insistence that the bonds between colonial and colonized are of the most intimate and benevolent variety. For in *The Rescue,* as in many Conrad works, a "family" is violently destroyed. Here, as in *The Secret Agent* (1907), the destruction takes the form of an actual explosion that annihilates Lingard's "children," Hassim and Immada, and demonstrates their "father's" carelessness.

The Lingard of *The Rescue* is a young man; the last book dedicated to his adventures describes the earliest days of his career. Already known as "Rajah Laut," Lingard is organizing an expedition to restore Prince Hassim to power in the country of the Wajo. His most obvious motive is gratitude; Hassim has saved his life. But Conrad gives his protagonist a whole series of motives, some rather mysterious, and several much less commendable than that of friendship: "He would wake up the country! That was the fundamental and unconscious emotion on which were engrafted his need of action, the primitive sense of what was due to justice, to gratitude, to friendship, the sentimental pity for the hard lot of Immada—poor child—the proud conviction that of all the men in the world, in his world, he alone had the means and the pluck 'to lift up the big end' of such an adventure" (p. 106). Most of the elements in this emotional compound are familiar and self-explanatory, but the sources of Lingard's "fundamental and unconscious" desire to "wake up the country" lie deep in the past, in his experiences in England.

The Raja Laut's memories of home are of bitter servility and enforced exile. An ex-trawler boy, he remembers England as a world of "poverty, hard work—and death," (p. 218). "If I hadn't been an adventurer," he reminds the haughty Mr. Travers, "I would have had to starve or work at home for such people as you" (p. 134). Condemned to perpetual inferiority and impotence in England, Lingard escapes to the colonies where he is free to construct his own world, one in which people will take account of him. His desire to "wake up the country," then, is an expression of his need to deny the identity imposed on him by the society of his homeland. Here Conrad, like Kipling, dramatizes the chain of cause and effect by which the colonized peoples are made to suffer because of the inequities of life in the imperial capitals.

Lingard succeeds as an adventurer, then, both because of and in spite of his background. He is impelled by a need to deny the debasing definition his society has imposed upon him, but he can do so only by first escaping beyond the boundaries of that society into a world where its constraints no longer operate. The new world of the colonies provides this freedom and more, for there Lingard's heritage as a European confers an instant superiority, makes him a Gulliver among Lilliputians. Strong in imagination as well as in body, he is able to convince the Malays of his power and to bend them to his will. But his success is provisional; it depends on his isolation from the constraints, psychological as well as social, of English society.

Thus the intrusion of the Travers party, run aground in their yacht at the very gate of Lingard's stronghold, is catastrophic in the deepest sense: it threatens not only Lingard's immediate plans to restore Hassim to power, but also his own long-range efforts to establish control over his own identity. The metropolitan English sabotage this program in two important ways: they challenge his estimation of his importance in the colonial world, and they remind him of his utter insignificance in the world of England.

Lingard's accomplishments, impressive in terms of his personal perspective and by the standards of the colonial world, appear unimportant to the Traverses and their metropolitan servants. When Travers's mate, Mr. Carter, first hails Lingard from the small boat, his manner is hardly complimentary:

> "What—ship—is—that—pray?"
>
> "English brig," answered Lingard, after a short moment of hesitation.
>
> "A brig! I thought you were something bigger," went on the voice from the sea with a tinge of disappointment in its deliberate tone.   (p. 28)

The point is that to Lingard the *Flash* is "something bigger"; she is his "perfect world full of trustful joy," (p. 54) and he is terribly proud of her. He is offended, therefore, by Carter's diminishing comments.

The offense is repeated when the *Flash* makes contact with the grounded yacht; Conrad contrasts Lingard's pride as he sails with the yachtsmen's rather disdainful assessment of the approaching brig. They see the *Flash* "with some disappointment, to be a small merchant brig . . . The general opinion among the seafaring portion of her crew was that little effective assistance could be expected from a vessel of that description" (pp. 54-55). Lingard himself suffers a corresponding diminution of stature; the Englishmen let him know that they consider him, the Rajah Laut, to be little more

more than a pirate. Thus suddenly and without warning Lingard's new world, the world in which he is a king capable of great feats, is invaded, assessed, and devalued by the very people who made his old world unbearable.

Why, then, doesn't Lingard simply expel them from his new domain? The answer is complex, for his failure to do so stems from considerations of immediate strategy as well as from psychological compulsions. (The psychological factors are complex. In *Lord Jim,* when Jim is dealing with a similar situation in the case of Gentleman Brown, Conrad attributes his fatal hesitancy to his need for an audience, or jury, of his fellow Europeans.) But the fullest explanation of Lingard's failure is that from the moment the Europeans appear they do not only devalue Lingard's new world, but also ensnare him once again in the chains of the old. The bitter memories evoked by their appearance and attitude shatter Lingard's self-confidence and reactivate his sense of impotent inferiority: "Their coming at this moment, when he had wandered beyond that circle which race, memories, early associations, all the essential conditions of one's origin, trace round every man's life, deprived him in a manner of the power of speech. He was confounded. It was like meeting exacting spectres in a desert" (pp. 121-122). Confronted by representatives of a world he has almost forgotten, by people too blind to realize that they themselves are no longer in that world, Lingard tumbles back like Kipling's Michele D'Cruze into the circle of the past. His sudden speechlessness symbolizes the failure of his power to maintain the new definitions he has constructed for himself. From the moment of meeting, he becomes more and more the prisoner of the old, confining language of his origin.

This reversion leads inexorably to the destruction of the world he has created, and at the climactic moment it is once again the loss of language that is decisive. Lingard lies mute at Mrs. Travers's feet while adversaries and friends alike—Tengga, Jörgenson, and Hassim—wait in vain for "a message" or at lease "some sign." When no sign is given, Jörgenson sets off the charge that blows all of them into atoms; Lingard, like a dying god, abandons his creation to chaos. In a minute, it is as if his whole world had never existed, as if his power of speech alone had conjured it up. And to an extent this is the case: Hassim, Immada, Jörgenson all act under the spell cast by Lingard's audacious imagination, and he directs their destinies until, seduced himself by more powerful spells, he abandons them to destruction.

But is Lingard's infidelity so much a result of sociological forces as I have suggested? What of the influence of irrational passion, of his infatuation with Edith Travers? The theme of the woman as seductive destroyer, alluded to early in the novel when Lingard and Shaw speak of Helen of Troy, is given greater emphasis than the political theme. Edith Travers, more than her husband and the others, is the immediate agent of Lingard's impotence and lassitude.

And yet there is a sociological component even to Lingard's passion for Mrs. Travers. By assuming toward her the manner of a courtly lover, he is able to act out his reflex toward submission, a reflex that has social as well as sexual roots. What is more, he can act out this impulse without shame, for the role of the courtly lover, unlike that of a servant, is one that even a king may play. So instead of playing the servant to the entire company, Lingard submits only to Edith. "I know my place," he assures her soon after they meet (p. 160), and from that moment on he allows her to give him the orders that he would be ashamed to take from her husband. But the act takes its toll; when he struggles to reassert his independence and superiority he becomes absurd: "I am master here after all—in this brig—as good as any one—by heavens, better than any one—better than any one on earth" (p. 178). In one sense, then, Lingard's infatuation appears to be a peculiar kind of sublimation. Instead of turning sexual drives into social channels, he turns quasi-social drives—the socially induced urge to submit—into sexual gestures. His love for Edith Travers, which seems to be the purely personal cause of a social catastrophe, is from this perspective an aspect of that catastrophe, a veiled expression of Lingard's inability to maintain his identity as ruler.

Thus Lingard, confronted with spectres of his past, surrenders authority on all fronts. Mrs. Travers occupies his heart and mind, Carter takes charge of his brig, and Jörgenson rules the stronghold in the lagoon. Each of them contributes to the collapse of Lingard's plans—Carter by attacking the pirates, Mrs. Travers by withholding a crucial message, Jörgenson by igniting the powder. Circled round once again by fellow Europeans who challenge his will and self-image, Lingard falls.

The explosion that announces the final destruction of Lingard's self-image also completes his betrayal of his Malay "family." But this betrayal begins at the moment when Lingard first encounters the English party, even before he meets Edith Travers herself. Thus Lingard finds, during his first visit to the yacht, that he has "forgotten, utterly forgotten these peoples' [Hassim's and Immada's] existence" (p. 135). He goes on forgetting them as the old English world reasserts its power over his consciousness until in the end their eradication takes an ultimate, physical form in the explosion of their stronghold. Recognizing that Lingard has become "the mere slave" of his fellow Europeans, the surviving Malays dismiss him as powerless and untrustworthy. Their attitude is foreshadowed in the reflections of Daman, the powerful Illalun warrior: "After all, it was perhaps a great folly to trust any white man, no matter how much he seemed estranged from his own people" (p. 296). The lesson of *An Outcast of the Islands* is reiterated in *The Rescue*.

Thus once again an attempt at a multiracial community ends, as in *An Outcast of the Islands*, with an explosion and a recoil into isolation. When all the parties converge, the outcome is an explosion of hatred that threatens utter annihilation. The survivors hurry to escape from one another, Travers sailing north and Lingard, due south. Once again Conrad seems to find hope for humanity only in distance and separation. But he has already shown the futility of such a strategy for survival; none of the parties fleeing one another ever wanted to meet. Now they pursue isolation again, but the reader at least must acknowledge that in a world both small and round their quest is quixotic.

 The Lingard novels demolish several of the flattering myths of imperial domination: *Almayer's Folly* questions the moral superiority of "civilized" to "savage" men; *An Outcast of the Islands,* the image of the benign imperial father; and *The Rescue,* the imperialist's claim to primary identification with his colonial "children." *Lord Jim* (1900) dramatizes an even more audacious revision of imperial mythology; it is not the natives, the novel suggests, who are dangerous children, but the imperialists themselves. When Cornelius, Jim's predecessor as manager of the trading post in Patusan, first insists that Jim is "no more than a little child,"[9] he seems absurd, for Jim has established himself as the fatherly ruler of the Patusan community. But as events unfold, Jim's crippling immaturity becomes more obvious, so that in the end Marlow must acknowledge that Cornelius "knew Jim well" (p. 230). Patusan, the type of those remote settlements where Kipling's youthful district officers achieve heroic manhood, is a world in which Jim's childish impulses flourish. The colonial world, a hothouse of exotic flora, is a hothouse for European dreamers as well, a place where fantasies thrive, obscuring in their luxuriance the plainer truths of unadorned existence.

Although previous critics, most notably Albert J. Guerard, have found in Jim's history a pattern similar to the one I trace here, their interest has been to extricate Jim's experience from its specific context in order to reveal its universal qualities.[10] My purpose is the opposite: to place Jim's experience as carefully as possible in its specific context, to examine the fateful interaction of his romantic personality with the colonial environment. By reintegrating actor and scene in this manner, I hope to illuminate an important political theme in this many-faceted novel.

Because my focus is to be on Jim's stubborn cultivation of his "Jim-myth" and on the disastrous results of this husbandry, I should begin by alluding briefly to his several virtues. Even his faults are attractive; his stubborn refusal to compromise his heroic ideal of conduct makes him an exceptional person, no matter what we think about the quality of his ideal. Nor is the ideal itself base, for as Guerard says, Jim's "childish romanticism may be preferable to a cynical realism,"[11] and it is infinitely preferable to the childish perversities of Cornelius and Gentleman Brown. Jim does not place solidarity with other men first in his hierarchy of values, but he chooses heroic models—the seaman and the paternal ruler—that emphasize the sanctity of communal service. He is a man of benign intentions, and he matters so much to Marlow because he is so nearly sound, so nearly, in fact, a hero for our times.

The tenacity with which Jim will cling to an image of himself as a fearless hero is foreshadowed in the events of his youth. Finding his ideal reflected in books of adventure at sea, young Jim decides to become a sailor. His initial success as an apprentice confers on him an easy sense of superiority; we see him, for instance, as a proud fore-topman literally and figuratively looking down on the rest of mankind. When experience reveals the distance between ideal and reality Jim simply refuses to acknowledge that he has acted less than heroically. A test occurs when a cutter from the training ship sets out in a gale to rescue the victims of a collision. Jim, "confounded" by the violence of the storm, hangs back and does nothing; yet instead of admitting fear, he rationalizes his reaction by applying the fair-play moral code of light fiction to the forces of nature. These forces, he assures himself, are no better than the despicable villains of romance. "Spurious" in their might, they have bested him only by "taking him unawares and checking unfairly" his natural impulse to heroism (pp. 6–7). Next time, Jim tells himself, he will be ready.

By imposing the ethics of boy's fiction on blind natural forces Jim demonstrates his unwillingness to abandon a self-image and world view that bear little resemblance to the truth of experience. His greater failure in the test on the training ship is not the failure to act heroically, but the far more important failure to gain a more adequate understanding of the malevolent forces in himself and the world. Instead, Jim continues to chart his course through the real world by fantastic treasure maps. It is not surprising, then, that he collides time after time with unseen obstacles. In the next crisis, the stoving in of the *Patna*, Jim cannot simply remain idle, for it is not some other vessel but his own that seems about to sink. Yet once again he is unready, once again confounded by a fear he simply will not acknowledge. He stands by as the European officers organize their own escape, and then, impelled by fears he has never considered, by motives he has never acknowledged, he jumps after them into the lifeboat.

His response, too, is the same as before; he rationalizes his cowardice by invoking the code of fair play: "He had been taken unawares—and he whispered to himself a malediction upon the waters and the firmament, upon the ship, upon the men. Every thing had betrayed him! He had been tricked" (p. 59). But this time the task of self-deception is more difficult; Marlow, watching Jim as he tries to preserve his "idea of what his moral identity should be" observes that he "would be confident and depressed all in the same breath, as if some conviction of innate blamelessness had checked the truth writhing within him at every turn" (pp. 48–50).

Although Jim can check the inward accusations of inadequacy, he is powerless to silence the accusations of his fellow men. During the inquiry and in the months that follow it, his self-image is challenged again and again by men who accuse him of criminal cowardice. Nor can he brood apart, as he does after the incident on the training ship; his notoriety follows him wherever he goes. Unwilling to accept society's image of him, yet unable to escape the imposition of that image, Jim begins to crack up. Recognizing that he cannot sustain the painful burden of his tarnished reputation, Marlow looks for a way to help him escape.

With Stein's help Marlow finds a way: the appointment to Patusan. By leaping out of the European community that has judged him inadequate into that remote Malayan settlement, Jim leaves "his earthly failings behind him and what sort of reputation he had, and there was a totally new set of conditions for his imaginative faculty to work upon" (p. 133). But Marlow's description of this second leap has ominous undertones. The observation that, although Jim jettisons his reputation, he carries with him his "imaginative faculty" suggests that the escape may be the prelude to a new disaster. Jim has not yet abandoned those fantastic charts of romance.

It is at this point in the novel, when Jim leaps at the chance to go to Patusan, that his unique personal history intersects in a signifi-

cant way with the history of imperialism. When Marlow offers Jim
the post at Patusan as a solution to his dilemma, he makes an offer
that was available only during a certain era, and only to a certain
group of men. When Jim accepts it, his experience begins to be
shaped by and to illuminate certain situations typical of colonial life.
He becomes, as his title suggests, an unofficial autocrat, close cousin
to Kipling's district officers, and his actions take on a representative
quality in spite of the unique events of his past.

Jim's motives for choosing to go to Patusan, though in one sense
highly personal, fit a familiar pattern. Like Lingard, he seeks refuge
in the Archipelago from a world where he has been condemned to
inferiority and insignificance. Again like Lingard, and like Mannoni's and Kipling's colonialists as well, he seeks compensation
there for a gnawing sense of inadequacy—by making the Patusan
Malays "dance to his own tune" (p. 178) he can restore the sense of
superiority and power, the image of himself and the world, that he
cannot sustain among his own people. Jim himself makes the crucial
connection; when Marlow offers him the chance to go to Patusan,
he replies, "I've been dreaming of it" (p. 144).

Patusan seems at first to conform to his dreams. His desperate
fearlessness and obvious rectitude, combined with the anarchic conditions in Patusan, bring him success almost immediately, and he is
soon the universally acknowledged ruler of the community. He is
an attractive ruler, too, the perfect image of a benevolent district
officer, or, as Jonah Raskin suggests, a dedicated Peace Corps
volunteer.[12] Unlike Kurtz, Jim prefers the work of creation to that
of destruction, the adulation of secure and happy men to that of
awed and terrified ones. Under his tireless cultivation Patusan, once
a barren battlefield of a settlement, becomes a thriving community
of secure people.

But Jim's fantasies flourish in the soil of his real achievements,
and in the end they choke these achievements out. Marlow observes
that both Jim and his subjects have an exaggerated sense of his
stature. Ironically, Jim's isolation, which is the result of his failure,
confers on him an appearance of superiority: his "isolation seemed
only the effect of his power. His loneliness added to his stature.

There was nothing within sight to compare him with" (p. 166). Thus Jim's heroic self-image still rests primarily on a delusion, but now that delusion is reinforced by his situation and confirmed by an entire community.

Jim himself realizes that he has become dependent on his position as Lord of Patusan. He relies on the worshipful atmosphere of his jungle domain as tubercular patients once did on the clear, dry air of the mountains. "This is my limit," he tells Marlow on the beach at the mouth of his river, "because nothing less will do" (pp. 202–203). In Patusan, the self-doubt he identifies as a disease can be controlled; "I've got to look only at the face of the first man that comes along," Jim observes proudly, "to regain my confidence" (p.186). The irony is that what Jim fears as a disease is in fact an essential ingredient of maturity. By protecting Jim from reality, Patusan only deepens the flaws that have already rendered him untrustworthy and unwanted.

Not only Jim but the people of Patusan as well are debilitated by the seductive climate of colonialism. Raskin, applying a needlessly reductive definition of imperial exploitation, argues that "Jim doesn't exploit the people. He brings no industry, establishes no British government."[13] A broader definition is implicit in Lenin's observation that finance capital stimulates an appetite for conquest and domination and in Mannoni's argument that "the 'colonial' is not looking for profit only; he is also greedy for other—psychological—satisfactions."[14] Jim's great need is for some confirmation of his sense of power and superiority. To attain it he must rob the Patusan community of some of its most precious resources.

Conrad suggests the quality and extent of Jim's psychological exploitation, and its parallel with economic expropriation, in describing Jim at the rajah's palace: "In the midst of these dark-faced men, his stalwart figure in white apparel, the gleaming clusters of his fair hair, seemed to catch all the sunshine that trickled through the cracks in the closed shutters of that dim hall, with its walls of mats and a roof of thatch. He appeared like a creature not only of another kind but of another essence" (p. 140). Jim monopolizes the sunshine of his adopted community, hoards the whiteness of all virtues, the energy of power. Beside him, because of him, everyone else is put in the shadow, diminished. In other passages Conrad describes the theft more literally. Jim has "the trust, the love, the confidence of the people" (p. 231); he has all the prestige they can confer, all the faith they are capable of, all of the confidence-inspiring adulation they can bestow. When Dain Waris, a prince among the Malays, tries to inspire his Bugis people to destroy Brown's besieged party, they refuse: "He had not Jim's racial prestige and the reputation of invincible, supernatural power. He was not the visible, tangible incarnation of unfailing truth and of unfailing victory" (p. 220). Nor is Jim unaware of his effect on the community. He determines early on to "make them all dance to his own tune" (p. 178), and when he achieves this goal he is delighted: "Those people had trusted him implicitly. Him alone!" (p. 163). Jim's appropriation of all honor, respect, and responsibility, an appropriation supported by the Malays themselves as the price of security, weakens the community and renders it vulnerable.

And so the stage is set for a reenactment of the *Patna* tragedy. Jim has reestablished himself in the childish state of benevolent egotism that was one source of his earlier failure. On the *Patna*, where 800 pilgrims depended on his skill, courage, and fidelity, "his heart was full of generous impulses, and his thought was contemplating his own superiority" (p. 15). Now the inhabitants of Patusan have abdicated all responsibility to him, and once again he reacts with a combination of egotism and generosity: "He seemed to love the land and the people with a sort of fierce egoism, with a contemptuous tenderness" (p. 152). His success is achieved, once again, "without [his] ever having been tested by those events . . . that show in the light of day the inner worth of a man . . . that reveal the quality of his resistance and the secret truth of his pretences" (p. 7).

Then Brown appears, and the test begins. It reveals the failure of Jim's resistance, the unconscious hypocrisy of his pretenses, and the fundamental unsoundness of the colonial society he has established. Jim proves to be defenseless against the rhetoric of his own rationalizations, and his actions belie his protestations of undivided commitment to the welfare of his subjects. The people of Patusan, for their part, show themselves to be slaves to Jim's delusions. They recognize, as he does not, the danger of letting Bown and his companions go, but they are too dependent on Jim's initiative, too devoid of confidence in themselves, to act without him.

Brown, trapped at the edge of the settlement he planned to despoil, appeals to Jim in two ways. He identifies himself as a brother in misadventure, as another brave man ill-treated by fate and misunderstood by his fellows. By so doing he tests Jim's "quality of . . . resistance," his capacity to withstand the seductive rationalization by which he has excused his own misconduct. Brown insists, too, that he has the right to expect certain things of Jim as a fellow white man, and that Jim must fulfill these expectations in order to prove his membership in the white community: "You have been white once," Brown growls with a terrible appropriateness of appeal, "for all your tall talk of this being your own people and you being one with them" (p. 232). With these words Brown tests the "secret truth of [Jim's] pretences," the veracity of his claim to solidarity with the people he rules. Jim, unprepared for both tests, makes the terrible mistake of identifying himself—an egotistical but well-meaning man—with Brown, an evil one. In an effort to prove himself "one of us" he affirms his solidarity with a vicious outlaw. He pledges to provide Brown with the "clear road" he desires.

Jim's conduct in the meeting with "the assembled heads of the people" (p. 238) that follows his pledge to Brown confirms his betrayal of the Malay community. As Jim enters, an old woman speaks the truth about Brown in his ear: "Are they not cruel, bloodthirsty robbers bent on killing?" Patusan's leaders share her view of Brown, and do not want to let him go. To win them over Jim first argues that Brown's party are only "erring men whom suffering had made blind to right and wrong." He knows this, he claims, because Brown and he have spoken "in the language of his own people." Then Jim goes on to assert what can no longer be taken for granted—his solidarity with the people he rules. He protests too much: "He declared . . . that their welfare was his welfare, their losses his losses, their mourning his mourning. He

. . . told them to remember that they had fought and worked side by side . . . he had never deceived them . . . He loved the land and the people living in it with a very great love . . . Had he ever advised them ill? Had his words ever brought suffering to the people?" (pp. 238–239). The leaders listen respectfully, but their determination remains unshaken. They refuse to agree to Brown's liberation.

In a community of men bound by mutual respect and obligation this would be the end of it. Jim would be saved from his blindness by the wisdom of his fellows, and they would be spared the danger of following a deluded leader. But Patusan is not such a community, for all its appearance of being one, nor is Jim ready to honor his obligations. He refuses to abide by the will of the community to which he has just proclaimed his allegiance. "Then," he says, when no one agrees with him, "call in Dain Waris, your son, my friend, for in this business I shall not lead" (p. 239).

These are the last words of a chapter and of a stage in Jim's relation to Patusan. The next chapter opens, as if after a moment of stunned silence, with a description of the effect that Jim's abdication produces. The clamor in the hall recalls the imagined clamor of the deserted pilgrims aboard their stricken ship; Jim chooses, once again at the moment of crisis, to abandon a group of people who have placed themselves in his power. Once again he becomes a criminal in Marlow's sense of the word; he commits "a breach of faith with the community of mankind" (p. 95).

Jim's threatened desertion—an actual desertion in that the course of action he imposes by means of the threat cripples the community—demonstrates conclusively the hypocrisy of his claims to solidarity. The people of Patusan have always been instruments to Jim; by ruling them, by becoming their lord, he has sought to reclaim his status as a superior being, a white man. He explains this to Marlow: "I must stick to their belief in me to feel safe and to—to . . . to keep in touch with . . . with those whom, perhaps, I shall never see any more" (p. 203). But simply because he considers the colonial world to be a compensatory one, and colonial honors surrogates for honors unavailable at home, he is ready to abandon his subjects when Brown, a European, offers him kinship. Jim's lover's reiterated charge against colonial rulers, "You always leave us — for your own ends" (p. 211), is confirmed here in a social context, as it is later to be in a bitterly personal one.

Just as Jim's threat of desertion reveals his untrustworthiness, so, too, Doramin's capitulation in the face of the threat demonstrates the decadence of the Patusan community he leads. The Patusan Malays have lost their self-reliance; they have projected all their powers, all their faith, onto an alien master. In return, they expect this master to assume all the risks, all the responsibilities of rule. Doramin dreams that his son Dain Waris will, with Jim's help, be able to enjoy the privileges of power without its dangers. Thus when Jim suggests that Dain lead an attack on Brown, Doramin gives in and agrees to let Brown go.

His capitulation leads, with fatal irony, to Brown's vengeful sneak attack on Dain's party, Dain's death and the shattering of Doramin's dream. These catastrophes spell the end of the community Jim has created, and destroy Jim himself. What do these final terrible scenes tell us about the imperial situation? Dain's death, so coincidental but so true to the logic of the forces at work in Patusan, harshly illuminates Jim's effect on the Malay community. Jim is responsible, through the vehicle of his evil double Brown, for the murder of Patusan's natural leader, the heir to power. The murder seems so plausible, I believe, because it merely completes a process of usurpation that has been in progress for years, the outcome of which is assured at the moment when Jim becomes "the virtual ruler of the land" (p. 166). Only one conclusion is possible: no imperial ruler, not even the most benevolent and protective, can both supersede and foster the natural leaders of the subject community.

Significantly, the act that exposes the full implications of Jim's rule also brings it to an end. Doramin is roused from his dependency by the destruction of his dreams. When Jim appears before him, the old man struggles to stand, as if by doing so he will reestablish his authority, affirm his capacity to rule: "The unwieldy old man, lowering his big forehead like an ox under a yoke, made an effort to rise, clutching at the flintlock pistols on his knees. From his throat came gurgling, choking, inhuman sounds, and his two attendants helped him from behind" (p. 252). Doramin's exertions have, for me, at least, an emblematic quality; his uprising, painful, enraged, and only barely successful, may be seen as epitomizing Conrad's view of colonial rebellions in general. Conrad's perspective is a deeply pessimistic one; it is Doramin, the vengeful representative of a shattered tradition, and not Dain, the more hopeful embodiment of an enlightened, synthesizing future, who finally brings Jim's colonial adventure to an end.

6

THE HEART OF DARKNESS

They will form themselves there.

CONRAD, "An Outpost of Progress"

When the doctor who examines Marlow on the eve of his departure for the Congo asks, "Ever any madness in your family," Marlow feels insulted; perhaps he is getting tired of hearing that he must be crazy to want to go.[1] But the doctor explains that his interest is purely scientific; he is conducting a psychological study of men leaving for the Congo, a study based on the hypotheses that such men must be driven by powerful irrational impulses to take such a risk, and that their personalities change drastically in the colonial environment. "It would be . . . interesting for science to watch the mental changes of individuals, on the spot," he admits, "but . . ." (p. 12). The doctor is interested in developing a psychology of colonialism, but he is afraid to risk his life for the information he needs.

Marlow accepts the risks the doctor refuses to take, and observes the changes of European colonialists "on the spot" in the Congo. He confirms the doctor's hypotheses; powerful impulses do indeed draw men to the colonial world, and powerful psychological transformations occur once they are there. Marlow's narrative, which focuses on these changes, provides compelling insights into the psychological maelstrom of imperialism. But Marlow pays a price for his knowledge; he, too, is transformed by his experience. *Heart of Darkness* (1902) introduces us to two radically different patterns of change: the transformation of acquisitive Europeans into robbers, murderers, and tyrants, and the transformation of a conventionally inquisitive European adventurer into a deeply reflective skeptic. The latter transformation, Marlow's, apparently reflects Conrad's sense of his own experience in the Congo. The parallels between fictional and actual events have been traced by many scholars, and Conrad himself suggested the deeper parallels when he remarked to a friend, "before the Congo I was a mere animal."[2] To what powers does Conrad attribute this capacity to transform animals into men and men into brutes?

A common interpretation of Kurtz's regressive metamorphosis is that Conrad intends it as an example of "reversion to savagery." Guerard, for instance, writes of Kurtz's "savage reversion" in *Conrad the Novelist*, and Fleishman comments that Kurtz "goes native." Meyer follows suit; Marlow, he writes, "is . . . struck by the realization that the potential for a regression to primitive savagery to which Mr. Kurtz had succumbed resides within himself as well." Meyer, unlike Guerard, who rejects the notion of reversion as "false psychology," employs the concept uncritically, with no sense of the questionable social and ethical assumptions it carries with it. By so doing, he simplifies and distorts Conrad's presentation of Kurtz's decline.[3]

The dangerous assumptions implicit in the notion of reversion are apparent in Meyer's discussion itself. Kurtz's metamorphosis, Meyer claims, renders him "indistinguishable from the savages"; to revert to savagery, he assumes, is to adopt the vicious traits of "savage" peoples like the Congolese. Meyer goes on to deny such peoples' humanity by equating them with beasts: "Under such circumstances," he writes, "regression to savagery can become a powerful temptation . . . In short, there are circumstances under which a man, even a good man, may be hard put to resist reverting to the beast."[4] Meyer's easy equation of savage peoples with beasts is anthropologically unfounded and morally irresponsible, but it does reveal the ideological elements of the theory of reversion. The theory exonerates European individuals and European civilization from the crimes of colonialists, and shifts the blame for these crimes onto the people who suffer from them. If the European acts brutally, it suggests, it is not because of any drives instilled or fostered in him by his own community, but because he has been contaminated by the brutal nature of the people he came to save. And if "even a good man" may not be immune to such contamination, perhaps Kurtz's answer—"Exterminate all the brutes!" (p. 51)—is the only feasible solution. In terms of the reversion theory, then, genocide becomes a legitmate form of self-defense.

I do not believe *Heart of Darkness* affirms any such vision. Kurtz's fall is portrayed with far more complexity and significantly less sympathy than Meyer's reading suggests. Marlow admires Kurtz in some ways, but he does not see him as a "good" man in any simple sense of the word, nor does he see Kurtz's savage passions and deeds as identical with those of the Congolese. In fact, while he clearly implicates the Africans in Kurtz's moral disintegration, he frequently contrasts them favorably to the whole "gang" of European intruders. Who are the victims, who the villains? Marlow seems unable to make up his mind. At times he casts the Africans as satanic corrupters of deluded but benign Europeans; at others he presents them as the innocent victims of satanic European invaders. The truth, he implies, is somewhere in between, in that hazy region inaccessible to archetypal moral plots and easy judgments. To share Conrad's vision we must follow him into this most uncomfortable region.

Kurtz, of course, is not the only colonial in whom Marlow observes psychological disturbances. His doctor provides a focus for an examination of the less extreme cases of personal disintegration in his cryptic prescription for survival: "Avoid irritation more than exposure to the sun . . . In the tropics one must before everything keep calm" (p. 12). The difficulty of adhering to this injunction becomes evident almost immediately. Everyone, Marlow included, acts irritably, irrationally, even hysterically in the

Congo. Fresleven, the captain Marlow replaces, is a good example; "the gentlest, quietest creature that ever walked on two legs" (p. 9), he beats a village chief almost to death in a dispute over two chickens, and proves the wisdom of the doctor's advice by getting himself killed as a result. Marlow recognizes the symptoms of a similar loss of control in himself soon after his arrival in the Congo, while shepherding an ailing European and a band of bearers on a two hundred-mile trek to the Central Station. The crisis occurs when the bearers desert: "An hour afterwards I came upon the whole concern wrecked in a bush—man, hammock, groans, blankets, horrors. The heavy pole had skinned his poor nose. He was very anxious for me to kill somebody, but there wasn't the shadow of a carrier near. I remembered the old doctor—'It would be interesting for science to watch the mental changes of individuals, on the spot.' I felt I was becoming scientifically interesting" (p. 21).

Thus even before he reaches the Central Station, Marlow experiences that loss of self-control and general rage against which the doctor warns. His description of the trek illuminates the conspiracy of irritations responsible for the transformation—the terrible monotony of the life, the claustrophobic isolation, the physical discomfort, the inefficiency and breakdowns inevitable in a situation where the master is an ignorant alien and his servants, virtually slaves, have little incentive but fear to obey orders. Marlow has "no end of rows" with the porters. When they rebel, he cannot reach them with words, because he does not understand their language; when they bolt, he cannot pursue them, for the landscape into which they disappear is unknown and hostile. His is an impotent authority, and an impotent rage.

The reaction of Marlow's companion—kill somebody—is typical of the other colonialists Marlow encounters. Fresleven takes out his general rage on the hapless chief, the pilgrims delight in the "glorious slaughter" of Kurtz's African followers, and Kurtz himself slaughters whole villages of Congolese. Thus the victims of the imperial invasion are made to pay for the frustrations of the invaders. The pattern is all too familiar, but it is not a pattern of reversion to savagery.

Of all the Europeans in Conrad's Congo, only two—Marlow and the Russian sailor—do not take out their anger on the Africans. The Russian seems incapable of anger, a kind of comic saint, but Marlow knows the feeling well. It is the Europeans, though, who evoke and suffer from his rage, not the Africans. When Marlow comments, "I was getting savage" (p. 23), he is describing his reaction to the phenomenal rudeness of the manager of the Central Station. Compelled to revert by the savagery of his civilized compatriots, Marlow lashes out at them with all the irony and sarcasm he can muster. Time after time in the course of his narrative he abandons his more important preoccupations to savor again the revenge he took on them for their stupidity and brutality. Marlow's choice of enemies is another indication of his reluctance to blame the Africans for the depravity of their European masters.

It indicates, furthermore, a basic difference between his orientation and that of the other company officials. Marlow, alone of the company agents, comes to the Congo without any intention to dominate its people or exploit its wealth. Like the adventurous Russian, he wants nothing from the Congo but an opportunity for exploration, a chance, as the Russian puts it, to enlarge his mind. Because his motives are in this sense benign, and because, like an ideal explorer, he has a clear sense of his ignorance, Marlow confronts the Africans with a minimum of prejudice. The others, because of their intentions, can see the Africans only in one of two ways: as servants of these intentions or as rebels against them. "Rebels!" Marlow exclaims when the Russian tries to justify the African heads around Kurtz's hut. "What would be the next definition I was to hear? There had been enemies, criminals, workers— and these were rebels" (p. 59). The Europeans' motives determine their definitions of the Africans, and the definitions—the Africans are either tools or traitors—legitimize their brutality. Here, then, is another source of colonial brutality that has nothing to do with the savagery of the colonized peoples.

It is in Kurtz himself that the whole question of imperial motives is most fully explored. Introduced as the embodiment of the highest ideals of the imperial mission, he turns out to have a good deal in common with his squalid companions in the company. Like them he lusts for ivory, but while they maintain the hollow pretense of legal trade, he organizes an army and takes what he wants by force. Like them he craves superiority, but while they compete for places near the head of the manager's table, he dreams of apotheosis and wins himself instead "a high seat amongst the devils of the land" (p. 50). While they employ the rhetoric of commerce to mask their exploitations, Kurtz, always careful to "take care of the motives," (p. 70), claims to be moved by the pure spirit of altruism. The differences in character are actually differences in imagination and energy; Kurtz pursues the same sordid goals, but with greater energy and, consequently, with less restraint. In the literal as well as the figurative sense of the phrase, he "goes farther" than the others—beyond the rotten fences of the Central Station, with its suggestion of crumbling but still surviving communal restraints, into a wilderness where there are no fences to keep him out and none to hold him in. Because he embodies the common aspirations at their highest pitch, his extraordinary fate illuminates the common experience and stands as a paradigm of colonial disintegration. It stands as well as an indictment of civilized motives in general, for when Marlow returns to Europe he sees its citizens hurrying, like less ambitious relatives of Kurtz himself, "to filch a little money from each other, to devour their infamous cookery . . . to dream their insignificant and silly dreams" (p. 72).

When Marlow interprets Kurtz's fall in these terms, he implicitly exonerates the African "savages" from primary responsibility. Instead, the responsibility falls primarily on European society, which legitimates avarice and domination, instead of instilling in men a clear conviction that these are dangerous appetites in need of constant surveillance. And so Kurtz, convinced of his own benevolence, comes to the Congo to grow wealthy and to play the role of god-the-giver-of-light to the ignorant blacks. His appetites and his delusions carry him beyond the last flimsy external restraints, and he discovers, with horror and fascination, the true shape of his personality, the true names for his motives. When his subjects approach him, he makes them crawl.

When Conrad gives this pattern to the trajectory of Kurtz's fall, he anticipates the findings of Mannoni, who observed the mental changes of Europeans in the tropics, but only a half-century after Conrad. Just as Conrad presents Kurtz as driven to the Congo by an experience of social and economic inferiority—"her engagement with Kurtz had been disapproved by her people. He wasn't rich enough or something" (p. 77)—Mannoni discovered that his subjects had come to Madagascar in an effort to compensate for feelings of inferiority, induced by the very structure of European society, by means of the easy superiority they acquired as Europeans among a weaker subject people. And just as Conrad dramatizes the terrible consequences that follow on the European's release from the protective custody of his own society, Mannoni warns that the European's personality deteriorates in the colonial world because of the lack of social checks against delusions of grandeur and arbitrary actions.[5]

Conrad suggests, then, that two of the colonialists' most savage traits, their unbounded lusts for power and for wealth, are qualities for which European society itself must assume responsibility. No Africans in *Heart of Darkness* are as voracious or as brutally aggressive as Kurtz or the other company agents; when the Europeans act on these impulses, they are exploiting the Africans' weakness, not emulating their "savagery."

Through much of Marlow's narrative, in fact, the Africans are presented with sympathy and respect. Describing the Africans he first encountered on the outward voyage, he remembers that he responded to them warmly as beings who "wanted no excuse for being there" (p. 14), whereas the presence of Europeans and their warships struck him as insane. The implication of this observation—that the Africans are peacefully at home, the Europeans violent invaders—is frequently on Marlow's mind as he recounts his experience, and it may represent Conrad's fundamental political objection to imperialism. Marlow probably makes this point most effectively when, in explaining why the country along the trail to the Central Station is deserted, he asks his audience to imagine themselves in the Africans' place: "Well, if a lot of mysterious niggers armed with all kinds of fearful weapons suddenly took to travelling on the road between Deal and Gravesend, catching the yokels right and left to carry heavy loads for them, I fancy every farm and cottage thereabouts would get empty very soon" (p. 20). The rhetorical appeal of this invitation to identification is powerful: the reader suddenly finds himself sharing the Africans' experience as peaceful victims of invasion. Marlow uses the same strategy to make an even bolder identification; he suggests that the sound of drums, "weird, appealing, suggestive, and wild" to European ears, may in fact have for Africans "as profound a meaning as the sound of bells in a Christian country" (p. 20).

The relative peacefulness of the Africans is asserted in another way as well. Describing the attack on the steamboat, Marlow observes that "what we afterwards alluded to as an attack was really an attempt to repulse. The action was very far from being aggressive—it was not even defensive, in the usual sense: it was undertaken under the stress of desperation, and in its essence was purely protective" (p. 44). In contrast to the pilgrims, the Africans seem to take no pleasure in pure aggression and fight only to protect themselves. The implication that theirs is a legitimate and restrained reaction to invasion is clear here, as is, once again, the suggestion of identification. Earlier in his narrative Marlow observes of himself, "I've had to resist and to attack sometimes—that's only one way of resisting" (p. 16). He presents the Africans' violence, then, in the same light as he has presented his own, and just as he denies his own complicity in the brutality of the pilgrims, he implicitly denies theirs.

Yet these same Africans are Kurtz's private army, his adoring subjects. Certainly they must bear some responsibility for his brutalization? Marlow suggests that they do, but not, it seems to me, for Kurtz's aggressiveness and lust for power. Kurtz brings these qualities with him, and uses them to compel the Africans' submission; he appears to them like the God of the Old Testament, "with thunder and lightning, you know—and they had never seen anything like it—and very terrible" (p. 57). Even before he makes contact with his people, Kurtz has cast off the robes of a benevolent deity and defined himself as a god of wrath. The Africans' submission is understandable; they have no weapons to match Kurtz's, no experience of any human beings like him.

Marlow sums up the distinction between the barbaric customs of
Africa and the more sinister brutalities of civilized men when, while
listening to the Russian describe the depraved rituals of Kurtz's
court, he turns his attention for relief to the heads drying on stakes
around Kurtz's house. "That was only a savage sight," he explains;
whereas the images of Kurtz's court are one of "subtle horrors"
(p. 59). When a man like Kurtz surrenders to his appetites and fantasies, it is not to the savagery of "primitive" peoples that he
reverts, but to a savagery that seems instead to bear the "subtle"
marks of a morally bankrupt civilization.

Yet Marlow clearly does implicate the Africans in Kurtz's
fall, does see them as savages. The heads on the stakes, while
"only savage," are horrible enough. (Kurtz's egotistical contribution to what seems to be a local practice is to face the heads inwards,
so they can "adore" him, rather than outward, as defensive warnings against intrusion.) And there are allusions to the psychology of
reversion throughout the novel. How are we to reconcile these allusions with Marlow's alternate vision of the Africans as victims?

The first allusion is also the most blatant. Discussing what he sees
as the analogous colonial experience of Romans in Britain, Marlow
follows a Roman Kurtz through the stages of his decline: "Land in
a swamp, march through the woods, and in some inland post feel
the savagery, the utter savagery, had closed round him—all that
mysterious life of the wilderness that stirs in the forest, in the
jungles, in the hearts of wild men . . . Imagine the growing
regrets, the longing to escape, the powerless disgust, the surrender,
the hate" (p. 6). In this passage wild men and wilderness are
equated with savagery, and both are implicated in the degeneration
of a "civilized" young Roman.

After this allusion, however, Marlow says little to suggest a
pathology of infection and degeneration until he begins to describe
events at Kurtz's Inner Station. Even then, he continues to offer the
alternative interpretation, reporting for instance, that Kurtz charmed
and frightened his African followers into submission. But for the
most part, he seems to reverse this evaluation, and to make Kurtz

the victim, his followers the satanic charmers. The wilderness, seen earlier in terms of its solitude, now becomes an actively malevolent locus of "brutal instincts . . . monstrous passions" (p. 67). And the Africans—particularly the woman who is Kurtz's mistress—are identified with the wilderness.

Employing the vocabulary of demonic possession and sexual seduction, Marlow presents Kurtz's degeneration as a case of temptation and fall, the Africans as devils: "The wilderness . . . had taken him, loved him, embraced him, got into his veins, consumed his flesh, and sealed his soul to its own by the inconceivable ceremonies of some devilish initiation" (p. 49). Here the evil forces are totally external and "primitive"; Kurtz comes to the Congo "hollow" and is filled with them. In a second form of the reversion theory, Kurtz possesses these forces already as part of his personality, but is ignorant of their existence until the wilderness—another great rhetorician in this novel of eloquent persuaders—enlightens him: "The wilderness . . . had whispered to him things about himself which he did not know, things of which he had no conception till he took counsel with this great solitude—and the whisper had proved irresistibly fascinating. It echoed loudly within him because he was hollow at the core" (p. 59). In this view, Kurtz's fall occurs because he, unlike Marlow, has no true "voice" with which to respond to the "appeal" of the wilderness; he has only the many voices of a natural con man, a brilliant hustler. But both forms of the temptation and fall imply reversion; in both Kurtz succumbs to passions that are part of the atmosphere of "savage" lands.

It might seem, then, that Marlow himself moves toward the view of the Africans summed up by Kurtz in the postscript of his report: that they are fiendish brutes in need of extermination. Marlow's analysis implies this evaluation, but his actions refute it. At the moment of his last contact with Kurtz's African followers, he has the opportunity to take part in the very project Kurtz recommends. Instead he sabotages it: "I pulled the string of the whistle, and I did this because I saw the pilgrims on deck getting out their rifles with an air of anticipating a jolly lark . . . 'Don't!

don't you frighten them away,' cried some one on deck discon-
solately. I pulled the string time after time" (p. 69). Marlow at last
makes an ironic sort of contact with the Africans on the bank, and
so succeeds in preventing their massacre, in spite of protests from
his fellow Europeans.

What are we to make of this dramatic contradiction in Marlow's
response? One way to resolve the dissonance is by reference to the
theory of levels of meaning: on the literal level, we might argue,
Conrad takes a sympathetic view of the Africans; but *Heart of
Darkness* is also a psychological allegory portraying a journey to the
Inner Station of the unconscious, and the terms of the allegory demand that the Africans be equated with primal passions. Alter-
nately, we might refer to Conrad's own personality, and follow
Moser and Meyer in suggesting that Conrad's sexual attitudes made
him particularly partial to and wary of the sensuality of non-
European women. This would help to explain his ambivalence.
Both these interpretations are plausible; both illuminate factors that
probably contributed to the apparent incongruity in Conrad's vision. But even on the literal level, Conrad's vision may not be so
contradictory as it seems.

Marlow himself suggests the most satisfactory synthesis of the
two "theories" of degeneration in his final reflections on Kurtz's
personality, when he speaks of Kurtz's soul as "satiated with
primitive emotions, avid of lying fame, of sham distinction, of all
the appearances of success and power" (p. 69). Kurtz's corruption,
Marlow seems to conclude, has two sources, one explicitly sensual
and identified with the Africans, the other aggressive and acquisitive and identified with civilized society. Two orders of
motivation, typical of two cultures, conspire to destroy him. But
the civilized order is primary; Africa's contribution represents a
"terrible vengeance" for Kurtz's brutal invasion.

If we compare "primitive" and "civilized" appetites in another
way, yet another synthesis is suggested, one in which Kurtz's
rapacious lust for wealth and power and the Africans' cannibalism
are revealed to be manifestations of the same basic motive. Kurtz's
desire to "swallow all the air, all the earth, all the men before

him" (p. 61), not only illuminates the sinister purpose of his eloquence — he's a satanic seducer himself — it also marks him as a can-
nibal gone mad, one whose appetite, unlike that of the African
crew, is beyond restraint and satisfaction both. Western civilization, viewed from this perspective, seems rather to exacerbate than
to mitigate man's worst impulse, his desire to destroy or dominate
his fellows. And the ostensibly benevolent imperial mission of in-
corporating other peoples into civilization comes to resemble, at
least in its motives, another widely condemned form of incorpora-
tion. This interpretation may reflect what Wayne Booth calls
"motivism" at its worst[6] — the effort to incorporate others may
reflect nothing more than a desire for community. But when incor-
poration proceeds as it does in *Heart of Darkness,* with violence as
the major tool and domination and exploitation as the chief goals,
then the identification with cannibalism seems plausible indeed.

In explaining the European's transformation in the colonies,
Mannoni alludes to the behavior of balloons: "Social life in Europe
exerts a certain pressure on the individual, and that pressure keeps
the personality in a given shape; once it is removed, however, the
outlines of the personality change and swell, thus revealing the existence of internal pressures which had up to then passed unno-
ticed."[7] *Heart of Darkness* contains many similar allusions, and dramatizes, I believe, a similar vision. Thus passengers and crew of the
steamboat find themselves almost airborne in the fog ("Were we to
let go our hold of the bottom, we would be absolutely in the air —
in space" [p. 43]) and Kurtz, who has "kicked himself loose of the
earth," makes Marlow wonder whether he himself "stood on the
ground or floated in the air" (p. 67). Kurtz ascendant sees himself as
super-terrestrial, a god; Kurtz fallen has the shriveled look of a
deflated balloon; always he is hollow. Throughout the novel, Conrad suggests that his European characters acquire their lusts for
wealth and power in Europe, where these lusts are also contained.
Then they come to the colonial world in search of freedom that will
allow these lusts to be expressed. They find it, and the sudden social
decompression causes them to "blow up" emotionally. They bully,

beat, and even kill the Africans on the slightest pretext, and their ability so to dominate another people causes their egos to inflate grotesquely, until they see themselves as gods. With this development the situation takes on a vicious sort of stability, for as gods the Europeans no longer feel bound by human moral codes, nor do they see their domination of the Africans as unnatural. Moreover, as humans playing gods, they enjoy reaffirming their new and shaky status by frequent exercises of arbitrary absolutism. Kurtz thus resembles a certain kind of *nouveau riche.*

But the stability of the colonial situation is only temporary. The pilgrims, blinded by their sense of infinite superiority, succumb to flabbiness and inefficiency; Kurtz, to the consuming fires of passion. All are corrupted by an environment they thought they had overcome. It is at this second phase in the process of transformation that specifically African forces intervene and take revenge. And if we do not share Conrad's even more than Victorian horror of hedonism and sensuality, we are likely to weigh the Africans' contribution more lightly than he. To do so, however, is only further to confirm a judgment implied throughout *Heart of Darkness:* the forces that brutalize the European colonial thrive at the heart of European civilization, which cultivates and encourages them. The imperial license should be revoked, for Europeans are not equipped to operate in a civilized fashion beyond the protective custody of their own communities.

We now know that it is not necessary to travel to the colonies to overcome civilized restraints; as the passion for wealth and power has been intensified, and as social restraints have crumbled under the force of economic and political pressures, men have achieved the same evil freedom without leaving home. Kurtz, with his insatiable hunger for fame and power, his sadistic love of suffering and death, his self-deification, and his genocidal solutions, anticipates uncannily modern authoritarian tyrants. Conrad prophesies the resemblance when he has a friend of Kurtz tell Marlow that "he would have been a splendid leader of an extreme party . . . Any party . . . He was an — an — extremist" (p. 74).

Heart of Darkness invites us to see Kurtz as a representative figure and to view his transformation as a revelation, perhaps even a prophecy. But what of Marlow? He, too, undergoes a transformation in the Congo, and although the novel stresses his lonely uniqueness, he, too, seems to be representative. Or, rather, I believe that Marlow has become representative as shocks like those he experiences, adjustments like those he makes, have become increasingly familiar. Over the last seventy-five years, more and more people have come to share his deep political and epistemological skepticism, his pessimism concerning human impulses and motives, his stubborn inconclusiveness, until he can fairly be said to represent an entire class of modern humanity. In examining the dynamics of his transformation, then, I want to focus on this question: why does Marlow's ordeal in the "primitive" Congo thrust him forward into precocious modernity?

First Marlow must be extricated from the process of degeneration that claims his fellow company officials and Kurtz. Marlow does become generally irritable, like them, and acts at times as irrationally as they do. But he does not engage in random acts of brutality against the Africans, nor is he bewitched by the charm of ivory. He escapes these degradations because he is immune to the appeals of power and wealth. The others come to the Congo in order to succumb; they are exploiters, acquisitive men. Marlow comes for different reasons. He is an explorer; his motives, inquisitive ones. Like the young Russian, he wants nothing in the way of material wealth from the Africans, nor does he want them to fear and adore him. Instead, he is anxious to understand them, to explore their country, and to enjoy thereby the explorer's intangible gratifications, the discovery of the unknown, the prestige of the exotic. The relative purity of his motives keeps him from changing as his fellows do; the transformation he undergoes is as unique as his reason for coming seems to be.

One way to sum up Marlow's transformation is to say that while he sets out to emulate the great geographical explorers of the nineteenth century, he winds up becoming a philosophical explorer, and a very modern one. What he discovers in the Congo is not so much an unknown world and an alien people as it is the truth about his own civilization. He encounters European armies, European companies, European communities, and, in the very heart of the wilderness, a representative of the finest European values. Moreover, he encounters them with their masks off, affirming by their actions the primacy of violent, acquisitive impulses in the community they represent. When Marlow joins the company he feels "let into some conspiracy" (p. 10); when he reaches the Congo he realizes that the conspiracy into which he has won entrance is that of civilization itself. The shocks he sustains, and the insights he wins, place him not with Mungo Park or Henry Stanley, but with the great cultural explorers of modernity, with the critical intellectuals, the artists, and the journalists.

Marlow's explorations expose him directly to an experience of disillusionment that most of us undergo, if at all, primarily at second hand, through books or films or speeches. Like those Americans who went to Vietnam out of a mixture of curiosity, idealism, and adventurousness, Marlow finds himself involved in a "conspiracy" that violates every value he respects and does so, incredibly, in the name of these very values. The rhetoric of the civilizing mission, and the slightly less pretentious rhetoric of material advancement, accompany him to the very heart of darkness, where Kurtz babbles about progress and the pilgrims dismiss his crimes as "unsound method." At each stage the discrepancy between benign pretense and brutal fact becomes more obvious, until at last Marlow comes to doubt all assertions of benevolence, all promises of progress. The best we can do, he tells his audience on the *Nellie,* is to recognize corruption when we see it, and to dig "unostentatious holes to bury the stuff in" (p. 50). Any more radical assault would be suicidal, for corruption has its roots in human nature itself.

The shocks Marlow sustains, and the discoveries he makes, are representative of modern intellectual experience. In *Ideology and Utopia,* a sociological study of this experience, Karl Mannheim develops theories that reflect directly on Marlow's ordeal. Mann-

heim focuses his attention on the "modern intellectual weapon" of
"radical unmasking," a tool developed by Marx, which operates by
"the tearing off of disguises—the unmasking of those unconsicous
motives which bind the group" to its programs and ideology.
Mannheim sees the universal use of this weapon as the most significant fact of the modern intellectual landscape; experiences of unmasking, he argues, have contributed immeasurably to the skeptical, relativist quality of modern consciousness.[8]

Marlow's Congo adventure exposes him to an immediate, concrete experience of unmasking, one in which he discovers for
himself the potency of motives uncovered systematically by Marx
and Freud. Like Marx, Marlow discovers that selfish and ruthless
economic motives are dominant in the spread of civilization, and
that these motives employ the rhetoric of morality as a mask. Like
Freud, he discovers equally selfish and ruthless passions in control
behind the individual personal masks of reason and benevolence. He
endures, in other words, the two greatest disillusionments of our
skeptical age, and endures them in isolation and without warning.

Paradoxically, it is when we begin to compare Marlow's and
Conrad's discoveries with those of men who never went to the
Congo that the importance of that journey becomes most obvious.
When Marlow's experiences are compared with those of Marx and
Freud, a common pattern begins to emerge. Both of these great explorers achieved their insights by changing their perspectives in a
literal as well as intellectual sense. Freud worked with the mentally
ill, who were unable to keep their masks in place; Marx ventured
beyond the internal frontiers of class to see how bourgeois civilization looked from below. Marlow's journey, which resembles Conrad's, carries him in similar fashion beyond the main offices and
drawing rooms of European society into a realm disguised by
rhetoric, cordoned off by distance and disease from public view,
where the rapacious impulses and brutal power of civilization can be
exercised without civilized restraint. The Congo, then, is far more
than a setting for Marlow's experiences, more even than a symbol
of European corruption; it is the standpoint from which Marlow—

and perhaps Conrad—first catches sight of the horror behind the mask. In other words, the insights gained by Marlow, like those gained by Freud and Marx, were won by strenuous reorientations and real risks, and quite possibly could not have been won without them.

Mannheim's account of the effects of unmasking provides another interesting indication of the essential modernity of Marlow's mental transformation. The first reaction of most people, Mannheim asserts, is a flight into skepticism. For some people this flight ends in nihilism: "They take part in the great historical process of disillusionment, in which every concrete meaning of things as well as myths and beliefs are slowly cast aside." Such men, he continues, become shut off from the world and renounce direct participation in the historical process.[9] Marlow is clearly tempted to move in this direction, and he does adopt a posture—dramatized by his assumption of the Buddhist position of meditation—of limited detachment. But Mannheim also points to another reaction to unmasking, one in which the process itself, and the skepticism it induces, come to be seen as "a means of salvation" because they "compel self-criticism and self-control."[10] Marlow starts down this path as well, and with considerable determination. A major theme in his tale, and throughout Conrad's fiction, is that only by self-doubt and self-restraint can a man preserve his integrity and act ethically. Marlow, recognizing the presence in his heart of dangerous and evil impulses, resists the temptations of the Congo. Kurtz, who deifies himself and lacks restraint, succumbs eagerly and is destroyed.

In "An Outpost of Progress" (1898), Conrad writes that life in the Congo consists of "the negation of the habitual . . . the affirmation of the unusual."[11] It threatens, in other words, what sociologists of knowledge call "the reality of everyday life."[12] In Marlow's case the erosion is even deeper; he is dislodged not only from the world of familiar objects and actions, but from the more fundamental universe of meaning of which that world is a part. He begins to doubt, in other words, the most basic categories and definitions of his civilization, the socially constructed reality embedded in its language.

Most of the European figures in *Heart of Darkness* are able to maintain the security of familiar habits and assumptions. The pilgrims,
ringed round by the rotten fence of the Central Station, dream of
ivory, of promotion, and of Europe; the accountant, in his office
within the fence, devotes himself to his books while a fellow European dies at his feet and Africans expire fifty feet away in the grove
of death. Marlow has only scorn for the sordid enchantment with
wealth that is the everyday reality of the pilgrims, and although he
respects the accountant's dedication to a task, his triumph of concentration, he comments implicitly on the narrowing of focus and
sympathy it entails. He, too, has his everyday world, his steamboat,
in which objects are correctly named and actions prescribed by
tradition and necessity. But Marlow is not simply a sailor; he is an
explorer as well, and thus although he takes refuge in the "surface-
truth" and pragmatic meaningfulness of navigation from time to
time, he struggles primarily to deepen his vision. This struggle
causes him to lose his hold on the grounds of conventional reality,
and sets him off on a vertiginous voyage through the fog. One of
the few certainties he salvages is that of his own ignorance and the
much greater blindness of his more confident companions.

Marlow's disorienting journey—he himself cannot get its spatial
coordinates straight—begins on the voyage out, during which he
begins to lose his grasp on facts and even impressions: "For a time I
would feel I belonged still to a world of straightforward facts; but
the feeling would not last long . . . Nowhere did we stop long
enough to get a particularised impression, but the general sense of
vague and oppressive wonder grew upon me" (p. 14). The problem,
as Bruce Johnson points out, is primarily one of language: "For
Marlow language is nearly useless in gathering meaning from his
surroundings."[13] One reason for this is the hypocrisy of the Europeans, who impose false definitions on things to justify their own
actions.

But there is a more fundamental problem as well. Under the
onslaught of new sensations, new experiences, Marlow's conventional terminology, the categories by which he discovers order and
meaning in the world, begins to break down. For some things there

are simply no words; for others words exist but seem only to destroy themselves in the act of application. The most eloquent example of this is Marlow's simple statement that "the earth seemed unearthly" (p. 36). Finally, there is the problem of establishing communication with the Africans. This too proves to be impossible: "The prehistoric man was cursing us, praying to us, welcoming us—who could tell? We were cut off from the comprehension of our surroundings" (p. 36). When Marlow finally does communicate with the Africans it is in an elaborately mediated fashion. His blowing of the whistle, which he intends as a benevolent gesture to warn the people away from the boat, is interpreted as he knows it will be, as a hostile sign. Marlow meets the same problem again, of course, when he tries to communicate his Congo experience to his friends on the *Nellie.* His "adjectival insistence upon inexpressible and incomprehensible mystery," which F. R. Leavis dismisses as an amateurish attempt at "magnifying a thrilled sense of the unspeakable potentialities of the human soul,"[14] also serves as a reminder of the limits of our vocabulary, and thus of our concept of reality. Similarly, Marlow's insistence on the darkness of his experience has epistemological as well as ethical meaning.

So Marlow, too late to join the ranks of the great Victorian geographical explorers, finds himself instead in the vanguard of twentieth-century explorations into the nature of reality. His experiences reveal to him the radical provisionality of his own everyday world and the assumptions on which it is built. In the end, he breaks out of the positivistic, self-confident conceptual universe of Victorianism into the relativistic, doubt-ridden world of modern consciousness.

This breakthrough, like his breakthrough into a demystified consciousness of human motives, has political significance. To recognize that the reality of Western civilization is not a revealed truth or a scientific fact but rather an artificial and provisional construct is to raise serious questions about anyone's right to impose that reality on others. It is easier to participate in the subjugation or extermination of recalcitrant others in the name of the one truth—religious or scientific—than it is to do so in the name of a truth, or, depending on how you look at it, a lie. Marlow's experience does not turn him into a champion of non-Western cultures, but it does convince him that communities, as well as individuals, should exercise critical self-restraint.

I have concentrated so far on the changes wrought on Marlow's consciousness by the experiences in the Congo. His transformation also has more social aspects, however, and affects his relationship to his fellow human beings. Marlow pays the explorer's price for his discoveries. This price is first articulated by the Russian, himself an explorer, when he tells Marlow that "I went a little farther, . . . then still a little farther—till I had gone so far that I don't know how I'll ever get back" (p. 55). Marlow experiences a similar sense of the possibility of permanent exile while pursuing Kurtz in the forest: "I thought I would never get back to the steamer, and imagined myself living alone and unarmed in the woods to an advanced age" (p. 66). Marlow does get back, of course, but only in the geographical sense, for the Europe to which he returns has been rendered fundamentally alien to him by the insights he has gained in the Congo. He wanders the streets of the continental city "alone and unarmed," appalled at the blindness and savagery of the people, hopeless of sharing his knowledge with them:

> I found myself back in the sepulchral city resenting the sight of people hurrying through the streets . . . They trespassed upon my thoughts. They were intruders whose knowledge of life was to me an irritating pretence, because I felt so sure they could not possibly know the things I knew. Their bearing, which was simply the bearing of commonplace individuals going about their business in the assurance of perfect safety, was offensive to me like the outrageous flauntings of folly in the face of danger it is unable to comprehend. (p. 72).

This passage captures perfectly the irony of the explorer's return, the bitterness of his realization that there can be for him no comfortable reclamation of the familiar world he has left, no easy sharing of the wonders and horrors discovered beyond its boundaries.

But what is Marlow to do with his knowledge and the isolation it enforces? The passage quoted above continues, "I had no particular desire to enlighten them, but I had some difficulty in restraining myself from laughing in their faces, so full of stupid importance" (pp. 72–73). Marlow's reaction is convincingly human, but it is a sign of his incomplete recovery from the ordeals of the Congo, not of his achievement of a new form of health. His response in another situation in which he has a chance to share his wisdom is even more disturbing. In his conversation with people interested in Kurtz, especially with his fiancée, Marlow once again withholds the truth. He is motivated, it seems, both by a sense of responsibility to a man from whom he has learned a great deal and by doubts about whether the things he has learned can be borne. Thus when Kurtz's fiancée tells Marlow that she wants "something — to — to live with" (p. 79), he finds himself unable to tell her the truth. His own condition — "It was not my strength that wanted nursing, it was my imagination that wanted soothing" (p. 73) — suggests that life may become impossible when the truth is known.

If we attend primarily to the story Marlow tells, we are left with the bitterness of this decision against revelation, in favor of lies and silence. Marlow leaves us with the impression that he has chosen, in despair, to give his support to the "conspiracy" of the status quo, with its eloquent lies and brutal truths. But this impression is by no means correct. Marlow, by telling his tale, and Conrad, by writing the book in which teller and tale come to life, speak their truth against the conspiracy of lies and illusions. Their publication of the things they have learned has several implications: that the truth can be lived with, that others have the right to know and the capacity for knowing, and that the knowledge will do some good. To follow Marlow's transformation to this point we must turn back to the beginning of the novel, for it is then that he chooses to speak.

In a dramatic and thematic sense, Marlow's story comes as a direct response to the reveries of the first narrator, who escapes from gloomy thoughts about the death of the sun by deliberately evoking a dream of imperial glory, of "hunters for gold or pursuers of fame" who have gone out from England "bearing the sword, and often the torch, messengers of the might within the land, bearers of a spark from the sacred fire" (p. 4). Marlow interrupts to tell his own tale, in which ivory-hungry pilgrims and an eloquent torch-bearer of progress figure largely as fools, madmen, and criminals. What are we to make of the juxtaposition? Certainly Conrad, if not Marlow, intends the Congo narrative as a vehicle of demystifi-cation, a vision of truths that will make the first narrator's easy ecstasy more difficult, and which will call into doubt his eulogistic vision of imperialism, British or continental. Perhaps we can assume that Marlow, his imagination triggered by the same sunset, the same gloom, has been seeking consolation as the narrator does; cer-tainly his first words ("And this also . . . has been one of the dark places of the earth" [p. 5]) suggest that he too has been musing on empire. In any event, he does speak out, with the stated intention of getting his audience "to understand the effect of [the Congo ex-perience] on me" (p. 7). He sets out, in other words, to induce the same profound changes in the others as he himself has undergone. (Two cryptic remarks at the end of his narrative—the Director's "We have lost the first of the ebb," and the narrator's "the tranquil waterway . . . seemed to lead into the heart of an immense darkness" [p. 79]—suggest that Marlow's tale has had the intended effect.)

There is a deep and, for me, a moving irony in Marlow's decision to speak out. Marlow points to it himself when he assumes the posture of a "Buddha preaching" and again when he refers to his conduct after previous explorations: "I had then, as you remember, just returned to London . . . and I was . . . invading your homes, just as though I had got a heavenly mission to civilise you" (pp. 7–8). The irony, of course, is that Marlow, who has learned to distrust any impulse to self-apotheosis, any aggressive civilizing enterprise, surrenders himself to the impulse, commits himself to the enterprise. After weeks of nihilistic scorn and silence, after a moment of paternalistic deception, he assumes the burden of the contradiction and speaks out. His action may be interpreted as just another sign of human irrationality, but I interpret it otherwise, as a pledge of solidarity, a testimony to the uncertainty even of despair.

Perhaps the best gloss on Marlow's decision is Conrad's statement, in his essay "Books" (1905), of the writer's responsibility:

It must not be supposed that I claim for the artist in fiction the freedom of moral Nihilism. I would require from him many acts of faith of which the first would be the cherishing of an undying hope; and hope, it will not be contested, implies all the piety of effort and renunciation . . . What one feels so hopelessly barren in declared pessimism is just its arrogance. It seems as if the discovery made by many men at various times that there is much evil in the world were a source of proud and unholy joy unto some of the modern writers.[15]

Marlow's decision to speak is an act of faith involving tremendous effort and coming after a period of arrogant pessimism, an act that affirms his commitment to an ethic of human solidarity. It initiates, ironically again, a new phase of progress or evolution, one in which human beings infatuated with their own wisdom and righteousness discover their limitations and the different wisdoms of others. The stance Marlow assumes, and invites others to assume, closely resembles that advocated by Mannheim, who echoes Marlow and Conrad both in his assertion that "what seems so unbearable in life itself, namely, to live with the unconscious uncovered, is the historical prerequisite of . . . critical self-awareness."[16]

Marlow's transformation anticipates an important change in English attitudes toward empire. In the nineteenth century, thoughtful, critical people were frequently enthusiastic partisans of imperial expansion; Thomas Arnold, the Mills, Tennyson, and Ruskin were but a few of the many who advocated commercial and administrative expansion in terms that at times resemble those used by Kurtz. But as the twentieth century opened, this same class, the artists and intellectuals of the age, increasingly came to believe that imperial rule, if inevitable in the short run, was an inglorious enterprise that deformed both those who ruled and those who submitted. Such writers as E. M. Forster, George Orwell, Leonard Woolf, Joyce Cary, and Evelyn Waugh all saw the imperial system at first hand, and all returned to write of its narrowness, blindness, and brutality. Their novels and essays record not only their own disillusionment, but the growing skepticism of many colonialists and imperial civil servants. Marlow might not have found himself so isolated in the company of twentieth-century colonials.

This is not to say, of course, that Marlow's critical vision prevailed overnight. There is ample evidence that men still go out to the non-European world to exploit it economically and psychologically. But the birth of the new critical self-consciousness, the ebb of the old imperial arrogance that Conrad portrays in *Heart of Darkness*, has continued in this century and has contributed to the process of imperial decline. The book is a profound study of the self-destructive dynamics of the imperial venture.

7

NOSTROMO:
TYRANNY WITHOUT TYRANTS

*Whatever manner of religious or civilizing pretext colonial policy
might have, it is always only in the interest of the capitalists.*

Resolution of the London Congess
of the Socialist International, 1896

In the Malay novels and *Heart of Darkness,* Conrad focuses on men whose relation to the socioeconomic forces of imperialism is deeply contradictory. Up to a point, Lingard, Jim, and Kurtz make use of these forces and act as their agents, but their ultimate goal is rather to escape from than to extend the zone of European authority. Sponsored by European traders and employing European technology, they set up private kingdoms beyond the limits of systematic European control and make no effort to modernize the communities they dominate. In a sense, then, they are the reluctant pioneers of a more systematic invasion they both anticipate and resist. Conrad turns to the depiction of that invasion, and of the men who lead it, in *Nostromo* (1904).

In *Nostromo* imperialism is capitalism abroad, gathering in "the outlying islands and continents of the earth."[1] The main characters in the novel are caught up in the economic transformation of Costaguana, a fictious Latin American nation. The chief agent of this transformation is Charles Gould, who owns a silver mine near the town of Sulaco. Unlike Lingard, Jim, and Kurtz, Gould makes no attempt to get beyond the boundaries of European influence. On the contrary, he internalizes the imperatives of capitalist society and seeks to extend its control. As a result, his gradual transformation is determined less by the fact that he is a colonial than by the fact that he is a capitalist. What he does in Costaguana, both to himself and to its people, is a function of his uncritical identification with capitalism.

And what he does, *Nostromo* insists, is anything but beneficial. The novel's assessment of the changes wrought by capitalism is crystalized in the "before and after" pictures of the San Tomé gorge. Before Gould develops his mine, the gorge is a tangle of creative and destructive energies, a "paradise of snakes" sustained by a waterfall that flashes "bright and glassy through the dark green of the heavy fronds of tree-ferns" (p. 105). Afterwards it is "only a big trench half filled up with the refuse of excavations and tailings." The stream has been dammed up and diverted to drive "the turbines working the stamps" of the mine, and the ferns have "dried up around the dried up pool" (p. 106). Instead of transforming the social jungle into a garden, this elliptical parable suggests, capitalism turns it into a desert. Capitalists may claim to liberate humanity, but in fact, as the forces they encourage develop, human energy is diverted from the cultivation of the social virtues; sympathetic, moral, and reflective faculties atrophy, and personal and social relations lose their human quality.

This charge against capitalism is a familiar one. What makes *Nostromo* unique in English fiction is the psychological and historical precision with which it substantiates the charge—its brilliantly concrete delineation of the process of desiccation. The novel is unique, too, in its elucidation of the dynamics of imperial expansion. But *Nostromo*'s brilliantly detailed political and psychological criticism of capitalism should not blind us to the less attractive elements of Conrad's political vision, his depiction, for instance, of the colonized peoples as inherently incapable of self-rule.

 Charles Gould, born in Costaguana to parents of English origin and educated abroad, persuades himself that only the establishment of powerful private enterprises — "material interests" — can redeem Costaguana from the kind of tyranny that broke his father's spirit and health. His profession of faith, in which he argues that the advent of capitalist enterprises will produce a "rift in the appalling darkness" of Costaguanan life, is deeply felt and even persuasive. Gould begins by enumerating his ultimate social objectives — "law, good faith, order, security" — then asserts that under the prevailing conditions of lawless tyranny these goals can only be achieved by the establishment of enterprises that require for their operation the maintenance of public order and are able by virtue of their material resources to "impose" that order. "A better justice will come afterwards" (p. 84), he concludes, in an acknowledgment of the limits of his proposal that further attests to the authenticity of his concern.

But while Gould's dedication to material interests is based in part on genuine social concern and reflection, it leads ineluctably to the exclusion of such concern and reflection from his subsequent decision-making. Having persuaded himself that the establishment of large-scale capitalist enterprises in Costaguana will automatically produce social progress, he feels no obligation to continue thinking in broad social terms. On the contrary, he concludes that it is his duty to concentrate all his attention on the operation of the mine and the new material developments it spawns. One sign of his deliberate withdrawal from socially conscious reflection is his dismissal of historical speculation. When the American financier and industrialist Holroyd suggests that the development of the mine fits into his vision of a world dominated by American capitalists, Charles refuses to think seriously about this possibility, and uses a version of his basic argument for capitalism to justify the refusal. "I make use of what I see," he proclaims proudly when his wife, Emilia, asks for his reaction to Holroyd's prophecy. "What's it to me whether his talk is the voice of destiny or simply a bit of clap-trap eloquence" (p. 83). If the pursuit of material interests will automatically generate social progress, then one is justified — or so Charles implies — in focusing on the material realities of the moment. The future, inevitably abstract, will be best served by this kind of benign neglect.

When Emilia, disturbed by Charles's refusal to reflect, asks him how he feels about Holroyd, he once again refuses to be drawn into discussion. "The best of my feelings are in your keeping," he replies, "but there are facts" (p. 72). Having isolated certain facts ("what I see") from their historical perspective, he now proceeds to take refuge in them from the voice of his moral intuition, which he deftly externalizes and dismisses in a familiar sexual division of responsibilities. Not only is he freed of the obligation to deal seriously with his conscience, but this obligation now rests with someone who is powerless to challenge his course of action in any concrete way.

Morally committed by his creed to ignoring the moral consequences of his actions, intellectually committed to the most narrow uses of his intellect, Charles becomes increasingly involved in activities that offend his innate moral sense. But this only reinforces his aversion to morally grounded reflection, so that when Emilia pleads with him to take an "ethical view" of their position, he recoils angrily. "My dear Charley," she cries,

> "it is impossible for me to close my eyes to our position; to this awful . . ."
>
> She raised her eyes and looked at her husband's face, from which all sign of sympathy or any other feeling had disappeared. "Why don't you tell me something?" she almost wailed.
>
> . . . "I thought we had said all there was to say a long time ago. There is nothing to say now." (p. 207)

By refusing to listen or talk, Charles makes it impossible for Emilia, or anyone, to awaken him to the truth of his conduct. Nor can he awaken himself; his refusal of public deliberation prevents him "from tampering openly with his thoughts" (p. 364), and gradually he ceases to "formulate his conduct even to himself, perhaps, let alone to others" (p. 316). As his power over the community increases, his connections to community—to its internal and external voices—are severed one by one. In the end, when the mine he has built to liberate the people has become "more soulless than any tyrant, more pitiless and autocratic than the worst Government," he remains blind: "He did not see it," Emilia realizes; "he could not see it" (p. 521).

In his blindness, Gould destroys both the intimate community he has made with Emilia and the larger community he transforms with his mine. His emotional and physical withdrawal robs Emilia's life "of all the intimate felicities of daily affection" she requires to keep her spirit alive (p. 512). The sterility of their life together is reflected symbolically in the disappointment of her hopes for children. Similar afflictions blight the larger community. "Material changes swept along in the train of material interests," observes the narrator. "And other changes more subtle, outwardly unmarked, afffected the minds and hearts of the workers" (p. 504). These changes are epitomized in the transformation of Giovanni Battista Fidanza—Nostromo—"the incarnation of the courage, the fidelity, the honour of 'the people' " (p. 515). In the early stages of the action, Nostromo's vanity, fed by his position as leader of the Italian workmen in Sulaco, is balanced by an active concern for the communities to which he belongs. He is not farsighted, but he does keep his eyes on his adopted family, the Violas, even when they are distant and he in danger: "All the morning," the narrator relates, "Nostromo had kept his eye from afar on the Casa Viola, even in the thick of the hottest scrimmage near the Custom House" (p. 22). And he treats all relations as if they were ones of kinship, guarding an unknown employer "as though he had been my own father" (p. 125). Here, too, his conduct contrasts sharply with Gould's.

For Gould and his fellows think of Nostromo only as an effective tool; they use him without regard for his intrinsic worth and without any sense that his fidelity to them is a matter of honor that should evoke a reciprocal fidelity. When Nostromo discovers their attitude, he feels betrayed, and his anger is compounded by his awareness that he himself has been infected with a similar carelessness. In his effort to save the company's silver from the Monteros he has left Theresa Viola to die without a priest and Martin Decoud to languish with the silver on the island. "First a woman," he reflects, "then a man, abandoned each in their last extremity, for the sake of this accursed treasure" (p. 502). Angry and ashamed, he comes to see his employers as oppressors and the mine as "hateful and immense, lording it by its vast wealth over the valour, the toil, the

fidelity of the poor". But even as he frees himself of any sense of
obligation to his wealthy masters, he adopts their corrupting ethos:
"I must grow rich very slowly" (p. 503), he resolves, having decided to steal the silver with which he has been entrusted.

With the "concentration of his thought upon the treasure" (p.
523), Nostromo becomes almost as blind and destructive as Gould.
Thinking only of himself and his treasure, he betrays his adopted
family, manipulating old Viola into guarding the silver, turning his
daughters Linda and Giselle against one another, and ultimately
compelling the old man to kill him. There is no *cordon sanitaire*,
Conrad insists, between capitalists and workers. They and their institutions undergo a similar transformation under the impact of
material interests.

In betraying his adopted family, Conrad implies, Nostromo destroys perhaps the last institutional sanctuary against the instrumen-
talist ethos of capitalism. For the Violas alone accept him uncon-
ditionally, as a kinsman. When Decoud speaks of "Nostromo"
("our man") in the Viola home, Linda retorts angrily: "The English
call him so, but that is no name either for man or beast." "But he
lets people call him so," Decoud responds. "Not in this house" is
Linda's answer (p. 232). In the family it is possible at least to dream
of not belonging to employers and the interests they embody. But
with the encroachment of material interests this sanctuary falls.
And again, Conrad suggests that it is not only the workers who
lose. If Gian' Battista is "our man" to Gould, Gould is "our man"
to Holroyd, who enjoys "running" him (p. 81). And Holroyd is
"run" by the economic forces he appears to direct: "We shall run
the world's business whether the world likes it or not," he boasts,
and then adds, "The world can't help it — and neither can we, I
guess" (p. 77).

The effect of Gould's program for Costaguana is to establish,
after much bloodshed and the division of the country itself into two
separate states, an unstable and tyrannical social order. The very
people Gould proposed to liberate are doubly oppressed by foreign
economic interests and the materialistic fetishes of capitalist ideology. *Nostromo* offers us, in fact, perhaps the first fictional portrait of

the establishment of the neocolonial phenomenon that political scientists call "dependency." Before Gould intervenes the Occidental Province is a preindustrial agricultural community; he helps transform it into a satellite of Europe and North America dependent for its continued survival on highly technical extractive industries, a mechanized transportation network of railways and steamships, and a steady flow of foreign loans.

The political implications of this change become clear when the aristocratic Antonia Avellanos and her uncle Bishop Corbelàn begin plotting to reunite Costaguana. Antonia argues that something must be done to aid the people of the other provinces, "who have been our countrymen only a few years ago, who *are* our countrymen now" (p. 509). "The material interests will not let you jeopardize their development for a mere idea of pity and justice," the disillusioned Dr. Monygham warns her.

> "We have worked for them; we have made them, these material interests of the foreigners," the last of the Corbelàns uttered in a deep, denunciatory tone.
> "And without them you are nothing," cried the doctor from the distance. "They will not let you." (p. 510)

Far from liberating the people from tyranny, then, the advent of foreign capitalists has enslaved them to an inhuman system and an inhuman set of values. Conrad overestimates the ability of capitalism to provide for the material sustenance of its colonial subjects, but he gives us a brilliantly lucid picture of how it brings them psychologically and socially under its domination.

But if Conrad's portrayal of recent Latin American history in *Nostromo* is anticapitalist, it is also profoundly pessimistic, antidemocratic, and even racist. In a key passage in the novel, Martin Decoud quotes Simón Bolívar to support his contention that political progress in Latin America is impossible. "America is ungovernable," Bolívar wrote in one of his last letters. "Those who worked for her independence have ploughed the sea" (p. 186).

Other characters are as pessimistic as Decoud. Dr. Monygham does "not believe in the reform of Costaguana" (p. 370), and Gould himself eventually concludes that the people are "incorrigible" (p. 364). Events in the novel tend to support these judgments. The Costaguana to which Gould returns has been wracked by decades of civil war and brutal tyranny, and his efforts to establish some stability produce two more wars and the dismemberment of the nation. Even then stability remains elusive; at the end of the novel the workers are rising to assert their own material interests and there are plans afoot to reunite the country by armed struggle.

Conrad's sympathy for the creole oligarchs—their values, beliefs, and the seignorial order they sustained—insures that his political vision will be pessimistic. From the creole point of view, as *Nostromo* shows, foreign capitalists were necessary allies in the ongoing struggle to keep the people under control. But the capitalists were also adversaries, for they, like the populace, threatened the social order the creoles wished to maintain. Too weak to rule alone, the creoles in *Nostromo* turn to foreign capitalists for aid, only to find themselves pushed aside and their country transformed into an economic and cultural outpost of metropolitan material interests. And the only visible resistance to continued domination takes a form—socialism—even more at odds with creole interests.

Nostromo provides ample evidence of Conrad's identification with the creole position. While foreign capitalists and indigenous liberals and socialists are condemned as barbarians, the Blancos and their allies are portrayed as decent, peace-loving men whose only fault is indolence. The social order they support with insufficient ardor against overwhelming opposition is portrayed as ideal; in the haciendas, the narrator informs us, "masters and dependents" coexist "in a simple and patriarchal state" (p. 88).

But if this is so, why is Costaguana wracked by endless social strife? To an uncommitted observer, such strife might be taken as a sign that creole domination is less benign than Conrad, and the creoles themselves, make it out to be. An examination of the history of the period also supports this theory. Under the seignorial order established during Spanish rule a small group of "pure" Spanish landowners, merchants, and government officials monopolized political power, the land, and the wealth that it produced. Their control was challenged periodically, but it was only after the break with Spain that popular uprisings became endemic. For this the creoles had mostly themselves to blame. They sought independence from Spain in order to be able to trade with other, more economically dynamic European nations. But to defeat the Spanish forces, they had to raise the general population. In the process, they found it necessary to suspend some of the restrictions that protected their monopoly on power and to call into question some of the beliefs that helped preserve their control over the larger population of mestizos, Amerindians, and Africans. Creole leaders, some undoubtedly in good faith, proclaimed their allegience to the ideals of the French and American revolutions. Promises of liberty and equality were made, and some mestizos and mulattos were actually allowed to cross the racial line and assume positions of responsibility in the armies of independence. But as soon as the wars ended, the creoles sought to stifle the new ideas and reestablish racial barriers. A few men of mixed blood, like the Montero brothers and General Barrios in *Nostromo,* were allowed to retain their positions within the circle of power, but in general racial barriers were reestablished, as Stanley and Barbara Stein point out: "Where the vicissitudes of the struggle for independence forced criollos to appeal in desperation to the lowest classes — to promise ultimate emancipation to slaves and to Amerinds full equality in the new society — afterward the new political elites were quick to reduce, even eliminate, this commitment to change."[2] In Colombia, the country most closely resembling Conrad's fictional Costaguana, the government decreed that anyone calling the people together would henceforth be guilty of treason.[3]

In a move that further increased social unrest, the creole oligarchs took advantage of their new power to institute free trade, a policy that served their interests as large landowners and merchants but destroyed the enterprises of local artisans and manufacturers, who could not compete with the flood of cheap British goods. This decision for free trade, taken at a time when the United States was maintaining tariff barriers to protect her infant industries, doomed Latin American states to economic dependency on Europe and North America. And by pauperizing the artisans and small manufacturers it turned that group into bitter opponents of the government. In the struggles that followed artisans, peasants, and creole liberals often made common cause against the conservative creole establishment.[4]

Thus in the very act of winning independence and achieving their self-interested economic goals, the creole elites awoke the antagonists who were to plague them through the nineteenth century. They promised the people political equality and economic relief but failed to produce either. They raised the expectations of mestizos and mulattos only to deny them equal access to positions of authority. They pauperized the urban and village artisans, perhaps the most dynamic element of the general populace. Given these betrayals, the general and continuing assault on creole institutions was inevitable.

The creoles themselves, of course, did not explain opposition to their rule in this manner. Instead they portrayed themselves as the defenders of "authority, order, and religion" against a godless mob of *gente sin razón*.[5] They argued, quite explicitly, that the mestizo, mulatto, Amerindian, and black masses were "people without reason, *gente sin razón* . . inferiors . . . requiring leadership, not education."[6] This argument explained both the popular rebellions and creole resistance in a manner that exonerated the oligarchs, but it also led anyone who took the argument seriously to the additional conclusion that Latin America could never achieve social stability, that it was doomed to an endless cycle of tyrannies and revolutions.

Nostromo projects this racially biased and pessimistic vision of Latin American history. The Liberal figures in the novel are without exception despicable men, barbarous, ignorant, and competent only in the arts of revolution and tyranny. The narrator makes much of their physical ugliness and calls attention repeatedly to physical features that suggest the presence in their veins of Amerindian or black blood, as if these features were sure signs of moral and intellectual inferiority. Thus the barbarous General Montero, with his "hooked nose flattened on the tip" and his broad, coppery tinted face, reminds the scornful narrator of a "military idol of Aztec conception and European bedecking" (pp. 120, 122). If he acts in an "imbecile and domineering" manner, the novel suggests, it is because he is racially unqualified for the European role he has taken on.

Speaking of the general, Decoud expresses the creole's racial theory of social unrest explicitly. "After one Montero there would be another," he proclaims, "the lawlessness of a populace of all colours and races" (p. 186). The anonymous narrator's assessments of the general populace, like his portraits of Liberal leaders, tend to corroborate Decoud's argument that Costaguana's problems are due to the racial composition of its population. The peons and Indios of the novel are the *gente sin razón* of Spanish colonial law; they know "nothing either of reason or politics" (p. 181). The more honest, brave, and patient ones support the Blancos; the rest, "violent men but little removed from a state of utter savagery" (p. 385), are the willing instruments of Liberal rabble-rousers. The novel endorses Viola's scornful assessment of the people — "Blind. Esclavos!" (p. 168) — but not his dream, pursued through years of campaigning with Garibaldi, of their emancipation. Thus the rhetorical resources of *Nostromo* are mobilized to confirm both Decoud's pessimistic prediction of endless strife and his racially grounded explanation of that prediction.

Fortunately, the concrete representations of life in *Nostromo* frequently undermine the interpretation of life it seeks to impose. In one scene, for instance, the old soldier Don Pepe responds to the visible signs of poverty and oppression he sees around him by exclaiming, "Poor Costaguana! Before, it was everything for the Padres, nothing for the people; and now it is everything for these great Politicos in Sta. Marta, for negroes and thieves" (p. 89). In his view, which is reinforced by authoritative characters and by the dramatic structure of the novel as a whole, black Liberal politicians have replaced the powerful colonial clergy as exploiters of the people. But the concrete descriptions of social conditions in Costaguana partially belie this interpretation of history. In the contrast between the hovels of the common people and the grand houses of the wealthy creoles, between the long lines of overburdened Indian porters and the creole gentlemen, "well mounted in braided sombreros and embroidered riding suits, with much silver on the trapping of their horses" (p. 88), is a strong suggestion that the creoles themselves have done their share of exploiting and that the economic system they support condemns people to poverty. But our attention is not called to this evidence by Don Pepe, or any reputable character, or the narrator himself. On the contrary, responsibility for unrest is explictly and implicitly attributed to "negroes and thieves."

Thus Conrad's ideological bias produces first a distortion of historical events and then, as a result of this distortion, a pessimistic denial of historical possibility. His failure to see the creole oligarchs as agents of the very disorder that threatens their hegemony—a failure that can be attributed in part to his own class background—leads him to interpret the stubborn persistence of disorder as a sign that Latin Americans are inherently incapable of acting rationally. If commentaries on *Nostromo,* including those written by liberal and left critics, have failed to question the validity of its portrait of nineteenth-century Latin America, it is perhaps because Europeans and North Americans have been conditioned to view Latin Americans in the same pessimistic and ultimately dismissive terms put forward by the creoles and by Conrad. As the United States' economic control of Latin America has produced ever greater political turmoil, we, too, have had to find self-exonerating explanations for our unpopularity and that of the regiemes we support. And we, too, have found it useful to conceive of our rebellious subjects as *gente sin razón,* and to view their protests against tyranny as proof of their unreadiness for freedom.

In the same letter quoted by Decoud, Bolívar, exhausted by the years of intrigue and war that followed independence, concludes that "the only thing that can be done in America is to emigrate."[7] While Decoud does not quote this part of the letter, he does attempt to follow Bolívar's advice. And *Nostromo* itself implicitly recommends this course of action. At the very beginning of the novel, in a letter to England, Mr. Gould, Charles's father, implores his son "never to return to Costaguana, never to claim any part of his inheritance there . . . never to touch it, never to approach it, to forget that America existed, and pursue a mercantile career in Europe" (p. 57). Charles's disobedience generates the main action of the novel, but this action tends ultimately to confirm the wisdom of Mr. Gould's unheeded call for disengagement. Thus even as *Nostromo* charges Western economic interests with the oppression and exploitation of Latin Americans, it presents an image of Latin America that has long been used to justify external domination and internal tyranny. And it invites its readers, who might imaginably be in the position to support the Latin American people in their continuing struggle against imperialism, to turn their backs on the entire problem.

T. S. Eliot once observed that Conrad was "the antithesis of Empire (as well as of democracy)."[8] *Nostromo*, with its profound criticisms of modern imperialism and vitriolic dismissal of popular movements, is perhaps the best evidence of the truth of that judgment. Judgment and novel alike illuminate Conrad's dilemma as a social philosopher. For it has proven impossible both to combat imperialism without appealing to the masses of people who live under its rule and to appeal to them in any other language than that of political equality and economic justice.

CONCLUSION

*Think a moment, old man. You and I were brought up together;
taught by the same tutors, read the same books, lived the same life,
and thought, as you may remember, in parallel lines. I come out
here, learn new languages, and work among new races; while you,
more fortunate, remain at home. Why should I change my
mind—our mind—because I change my sky? Why should I and the
few hundred Englishmen in my service become unreasonable, prejudiced fossils, while you and your newer friends alone remain bright
and open-minded?*

Kipling, "The Enlightenments of Pagett, M.P."

The changes take place inside, you know.

Conrad, *Heart of Darkness*

Both Kipling and Conrad are sure that some change does occur when Europeans step beyond the boundaries of their
own culture into the new world of the Empire, and both appropriate that change as subject for their fiction. Like Orde, the speaker
in "The Enlightenments of Pagett, M.P.," both authors insist that
the transformation is one that any European might undergo. But
while Kipling makes this point in order to stress the essential ra-
tionality of the change—in order, that is, to justify it—Conrad un-
covers the European roots of the colonialist's metamorphosis to
show that "all Europe contributed to the making of Kurtz."[1]

In dramatizing their colonial characters' transformations, Kipling
and Conrad win our sympathy for men it is easy and fashionable to
dislike. But they also confirm, though Kipling does so unwittingly,

the charges leveled against these men: that they are bent more on domination than on education, that they cherish superiority more than brotherhood, that they approve of manipulation and coercion as the tools of rule, and that they enjoy using them. Kipling wins our sympathy for his Anglo-Indian heroes by dramatizing their sufferings and pointing out the massiveness of the forces that shaped them to the imperial mold. Reading his stories, we realize how much of their experience confirms the authoritarian view of the world as a place structured in dyads of dominance and submission, obedience and isolation, power and pain. Kipling shows us, in other words, that his contemporaries in the imperial service did not merely choose such a world view to justify their activities in India. Although they may have affirmed the authoritarian perspective partly for this reason, they had ample cause in their own experiences as children and adults to see the world in just these terms.

The problem is that Kipling himself shares their perspective; he accepts the psychological and social situation perceived by the imperial servant as delimiting the boundaries of human possibility. As a result, his works often read like the testimony of a friendly witness whose efforts backfire because he sees nothing wrong in the criminal actions of the accused. Kipling dramatizes the imperialists' lust for absolute authority, love of domination, and practice of the wiles of fraternal despotism as if these were the impulses and actions of healthy men.

Because we are still partially immersed in the society, the period, and perhaps even the class to which Kipling belonged, his vision of the world may win some assent. But we know now, or some of us believe, that although the urge to dominate has probably always been part of humans' psychological makeup, imperialism nurtures this trait above all others. Thus we see Kipling and the imperial figures he portrays locked in a vision and experience of the world that made their fear, their lust for power, their violence, and perhaps even their downfall inevitable. But at the same time we rejoice when people in similar situations—Americans in Vietnam, Portuguese in Africa—recognize that the only way to break out of their own slavery is to make common cause with the peoples they have been trained to oppress.

Conrad obtains our sympathy for his colonial despots not by focusing on their sufferings but by dramatizing the dreams that impel them in their projects of domination. Lingard, Jim, and Kurtz imagine themselves as benign, omniscient fathers of loving communities, and Lingard and Jim achieve for a time some semblance of that dream. Because the dream is a familiar one, in both the conventional and the etymological sense of the word, we are all likely to have entertained it ourselves. In short, it is impossible to dismiss the imperialist as some satanic other with whom we have no kinship.

But kinship in Conrad is never cause for uncritical approval. Unlike Kipling, Conrad does not share his colonial protagonists' belief in the viability of paternal despotism; he encompasses their vision in a larger critical view. Lingard, Jim, and even Kurtz, he shows us, are aware of only the most benign of the several motives impelling their search for power. Childish egotism, intolerance of others, appetites for dominance, status, and wealth also determine their course. Similarly, while they believe that their impact on the colonized peoples is purely constructive, Conrad shows us that their actions are psychologically and economically exploitative. And he recommends through Marlow, his wisest character, a withdrawal from imperial domination that has won more and more advocates in this century.

NOTES

INDEX

NOTES

There is as yet no standard edition of Kipling's works. I have used the *Outward Bound Edition*, 30 volumes (New York: Charles Scribner's Sons, 1897–1923) whenever possible. Unless otherwise noted, citations to Conrad's work refer to the *Collected Edition of the Works of Joseph Conrad*, 21 volumes (London: J. M. Dent and Sons, 1946–1955). Pagination in this edition is identical with the Dent Uniform Edition (1923–1928) and with the Canterbury Edition (Garden City, N.Y.: Doubleday, Page, 1924–1926).

Introduction

1. James Payne, "Our Note Book," *Illustrated London News*, 112 (1898), 172; quoted in David Thorburn, *Conrad's Romanticism* (New Haven: Yale University Press, 1974), p. 4. Although Kipling and Conrad were frequently compared by contemporary reviewers and although they lived not far from one another in Kent for several years, they apparently never met. Conrad, who refers briefly to Kipling in several letters, did prepare an article on his work in 1898, but it was never printed and seems to have been lost. Edmund Bojarski's article, "A Conversation with Kipling on Conrad," *Kipling Journal*, 34 (June 1967), gives us some sense of Kipling's attitude toward his fellow author, reports on their one known epistolary contact, and cites their few published references to one another.

2. Thorburn, *Romanticism*, p. 4.

3. Joseph Conrad, *Heart of Darkness*, ed. Robert Kimbrough (1902; reprint ed., New York: W. W. Norton, 1971), p. 12.

4. George Orwell, "Rudyard Kipling" (1942); reprinted in Andrew Rutherford, ed., *Kipling's Mind and Art* (Stanford: Stanford University Press, 1964), p. 74.

5. Conrad, *Heart of Darkness*, p. 50.

6. Rudyard Kipling, "William the Conqueror," in *The Day's Work: Part I* (1893; reprint ed., New York: Charles Scribner's Sons, 1899), p. 250.

7. Ibid., p. 230.

8. Rudyard Kipling, "The Totem," in *Songs from Books and Later Songs from Books* (New York: Doubleday, Doran, 1941), p. 392.

9. Joseph Conrad, *The Nigger of the "Narcissus"* (1898), pp. xi–xii.

10. Conrad, *Heart of Darkness,* p. 34.

1. Kipling's Empire

1. Raymond Williams, *George Orwell* (New York: Viking Press, 1971), p. 14.

2. George Orwell, *The Road to Wigan Pier* (1937); quoted in Williams, *Orwell,* p. 13.

3. Rudyard Kipling, "Values in Life," in *A Book of Words* (1907; reprint ed., New York: Charles Scribner's Sons, 1928), p. 24.

4. See T. W. Adorno et al., *The Authoritarian Personality* (1950; reprint ed., New York: W. W. Norton, 1969); Erich Fromm, *Escape from Freedom* (1941; reprint ed., New York: Avon Books, 1969). Edmund Wilson makes the connection between Kipling's painful childhood and his authoritarian vision in his essay "The Kipling that Nobody Read" (1941); reprinted in Rutherford, *Kipling's Mind and Art,* pp. 17–69. But Wilson does not note that Kipling's experiences were in many respects typical for members of the imperial service elite, as were the conclusions he drew from them.

5. Alice Fleming, "Some Childhood Memories of Rudyard Kipling," *Chamber's Journal,* 8th ser., 8 (1939), 171; quoted in Wilson, "Kipling that Nobody Read," p. 19.

6. Rudyard Kipling, "Gow's Watch," in *Rudyard Kipling's Verse: Definitive Edition* (New York: Doubleday, 1959).

7. Rudyard Kipling, *Something of Myself* (New York: Charles Scribner's Sons, 1937); see pp. 8, 17, 18.

8. Ibid., pp. 8, 11, 12.

9. Ibid., p. 16.

10. Rudyard Kipling, "Baa Baa, Black Sheep," in *Under the Deodars and Other Stories* (1897; reprint ed., New York: Charles Scribner's Sons, 1899), p. 330. Subsequent references to this edition appear in the text.

11. W. J. Wilkins, *Daily Life and Work in India* (London, 1887); quoted in Louis Cornell, *Kipling in India* (New York: St. Martin's Press, 1966), pp. 5–6.

12. Kipling, *Something of Myself,* pp. 24, 26.

13. L. C. Dunsterville, *Stalky's Reminiscences* (New York: Macmillan, 1928), p. 31.

14. Kipling, *Something of Myself,* pp. 40–41.

15. Ibid., p. 90.

16. Rudyard Kipling, "At the End of the Passage," in *The Phantom Rickshaw and Other Stories* (1897; reprint ed., New York: Charles Scribner's Sons, 1899), p. 345.

17. Rudyard Kipling, "The Widow at Windsor" and "The Widow's Party," in *Departmental Ditties and Ballads and Barrack-Room Ballads* (New York: Doubleday and McClure, 1899), pp. 179, 197.

18. Michael Edwardes, *Bound to Exile* (New York: Praeger, 1969), pp. 164–165.

19. Rudyard Kipling, "The Drums of the Fore and Aft," in *Soldiers Three and Military Tales: Part II* (1897; reprint ed., New York: Charles Scribner's Sons, 1899), p. 478.

20. Rudyard Kipling, "The Three Musketeers," in *Soldiers Three and Military Tales: Part I* (1897; reprint ed., New York: Charles Scribner's Sons, 1899), p. 1.

21. Rudyard Kipling, "On Greenhow Hill," ibid., p. 209. Subsequent references to this edition appear in the text.

22. Fromm, *Escape from Freedom,* p. 207.

23. Rudyard Kipling, "Loot," in *Departmental Ditties,* pp. 172–173.

24. Rudyard Kipling, *Stalky and Co.* (1899; reprint ed., New York: Doubleday, Page, 1914), p. 330.

25. Rudyard Kipling, "The Lost Legion," in *Departmental Ditties,* p. 74.

26. Rudyard Kipling, *The Naulahka* (1891; reprint ed., New York: Charles Scribner's Sons, 1899), p. 361. Subsequent references to this edition appear in the text.

27. Rudyard Kipling, "His Chance in Life," in *Plain Tales from the Hills* (1888; reprint ed., New York: Charles Scribner's Sons, 1899), p. 88.

28. Rudyard Kipling, "The Man Who Would Be King," in *Phantom Rickshaw,* pp. 39–97.

29. Rudyard Kipling, "On the City Wall," in *In Black and White* (1888; reprint ed., New York: Charles Scribner's Sons, 1899), p. 305.

30. Rudyard Kipling, "The Head of the District," in *In Black and White,* pp. 172–173.

31. Rudyard Kipling, "The Judgment of Dungara," in *In Black and White.* Subsequent references to this edition appear in the text.

32. Rudyard Kipling, "The Galley-Slave," in *Departmental Ditties,* p. 151.

33. See Edward Thompson and G. T. Garratt, *Rise and Fulfillment of British Rule in India* (London: Macmillan, 1934), pp. 461–483.

34. See Francis Hutchins, *The Illusion of Permanence: British Imperialism in India* (Princeton: Princeton University Press, 1967), pp. 153–172.

35. Rudyard Kipling, "The Enlightenments of Pagett, M.P.," in *In Black and White,* pp. 357–358.

2. Unbearable Burdens

1. Kipling, "End of the Passage," p. 330.

2. Rudyard Kipling, "Gentlemen-Rankers," in *Departmental Ditties,* p. 205.

3. See Rudyard Kipling, "Thrown Away," in *Plain Tales,* p. 17.

4. Rudyard Kipling, "The Strange Ride of Morrowbie Jukes," in *Phantom Rickshaw,* pp. 216–217. Subsequent references to this edition appear in the text.

5. Jonah Raskin, *The Mythology of Imperialism* (New York: Random House, 1971), p. 73.

6. Rudyard Kipling, "The Phantom Rickshaw," in *Phantom Rickshaw*, pp. 13–14.

7. Rudyard Kipling, "The Return of Imray," in *Phantom Rickshaw*, p. 284. Subsequent references to this edition appear in the text.

8. Kipling, "Phantom Rickshaw," p. 3.

9. Kipling, "End of the Passage," p. 357.

10. Rudyard Kipling, "The Madness of Private Ortheris," in *Soldiers Three: Part I*, pp. 24–25. Subsequent references to this edition appear in the text.

11. Rudyard Kipling, "Beyond the Pale," in *Plain Tales*, p. 189.

12. Ibid., p. 194.

13. Rudyard Kipling, "To Be Filed for Reference," in *Plain Tales*, p. 345.

14. C. E. Carrington, *The Life of Rudyard Kipling* (New York: Doubleday, 1955), pp. 61–62, 64.

15. Kipling, *Something of Myself*, pp. 52–53.

16. Kipling, "Beyond the Pale," p. 189.

17. Cornell, *Kipling in India*, p. 139.

18. Ibid.

19. Kipling, "Beyond the Pale," p. 189.

20. Kipling, "To Be Filed," p. 341.

21. Rudyard Kipling, "Miss Youghal's Sais," in *Plain Tales*, p. 33.

22. Rudyard Kipling, "Lispeth," in *Plain Tales*, p. 7.

23. Ibid., p. 8.

24. Kipling, "Chance in Life," p. 84. Subsequent references to this edition appear in the text.

25. James Fitzjames Stephen to *Times* (London), March 1, 1883; quoted in Eric Stokes, *The English Utilitarians and India* (Oxford, Oxford University Press, 1959), p. 288.

3. Lifting the Burden

1. See Kipling, "Thrown Away," p. 17.

2. Rudyard Kipling, "The Mark of the Beast," in *Phantom Rickshaw*, p. 175.

3. Rudyard Kipling, *The Jungle Book* (1894; reprint ed., New York: Charles Scribner's Sons, 1899), pp. 4–5. Subsequent references to this edition appear in the text.

4. Rudyard Kipling, "The Son of His Father," in *Day's Work: Part I*, p. 277. Subsequent references to this edition appear in the text.

5. O. Mannoni, *Prospero and Caliban: The Psychology of Colonization*, trans. Pamela Powesland (New York: Praeger, 1964), pp. 126–127.

6. Ibid., p. 128.

7. Ezekiel Mphahlele, "Censorship in South Africa," in *Voices in the Whirlwind* (New York: Hill and Wang, 1967), p. 213.

8. Mark Kinkead-Weekes, "Vision in Kipling's Novels," in Rutherford, *Kipling's Mind and Art*, p. 233.

9. J. M. S. Tompkins, *The Art of Rudyard Kipling* (London: Methuen, 1959), p. 23; Kinkead-Weekes, "Vision in Kipling's Novels," p. 216.

10. Rudyard Kipling, *Kim* (1901; reprint ed., New York: Charles Scribner's Sons, 1913), p. 238. Subsequent references to this edition appear in the text.

11. Lionel Trilling, "Kipling," in Rutherford, *Kipling's Mind and Art,* p. 88.

12. Kinkead-Weekes, "Vision in Kipling's Novels," p. 217.

4. Joseph Conrad

1. Raskin, *Mythology,* p. 128.

2. Joseph Conrad, "Poland Revisited" (1915); reprinted in *Notes on Life and Letters* (1921), p. 168.

3. Quoted in Zdzislaw Najder, ed., *Conrad's Polish Background* (London: Oxford University Press, 1964), p. 11.

4. Bernard Meyer, *Joseph Conrad: A Psychoanalytic Biography* (Princeton: Princeton University Press, 1967), pp. 85-86.

5. Ibid., p. 288.

6. Korzeniowski to Jan Zagórski, 1865, in Jean Aubry, *Joseph Conrad: Life and Letters,* 2 vols. (New York: Doubleday, Page, 1927), I: 16.

7. Joseph Conrad, *A Personal Record* (1912), p. 31.

8. Meyer, *Conrad,* p. 281.

9. Avrom Fleishman, *Conrad's Politics* (Baltimore: Johns Hopkins University Press, 1967).

10. Ibid., pp. 4, 111.

11. See Jocelyn Baines, *Joseph Conrad: A Critical Biography* (1960; reprint ed., New York: McGraw-Hill, 1967); John Gordan, *Joseph Conrad: The Making of a Novelist* (1940; reprint ed., New York: Russell and Russell, 1963); Norman Sherry, *Conrad's Eastern World* (Cambridge: Cambridge University Press, 1966); idem, *Conrad's Western World* (Cambridge: Cambridge University Press, 1971).

12. Sherry, *Conrad's Eastern World,* pp. 102-107.

13. Quoted in Thomas Moser, " 'The Rescuer' Manuscript: A Key to Conrad's Development—and Decline," in *Harvard Library Bulletin,* 10 (1956), 337.

14. Conrad to E. L. Sanderson, October 12, 1899, in Aubry, *Life and Letters,* I: 283-284.

15. Conrad, *Personal Record,* p. xx.

16. Conrad, *Heart of Darkness,* p. 50.

17. Conrad, *Personal Record,* p. xx.

18. Alan Sandison, *The Wheel of Empire* (New York: St. Martin's Press, 1967), p. 62.

19. Conrad to Graham, May 1, 1898, in Joseph Conrad, *Joseph Conrad's Letters to Cunninghame Graham,* ed. C. T. Watts (Cambridge: Cambridge University Press, 1969), pp. 84-85.

20. Joseph Conrad, "Autocracy and War" (1905), in *Notes,* p. 106.

21. Ibid., p. 112.

22. Ibid., pp. 107–108.

23. Conrad to Graham, February 8, 1899, in Conrad's *Letters to Graham,* p. 117.

24. Conrad to Graham, 1898, in Conrad, *Letters to Graham,* p. 68.

25. Joseph Conrad, "The Crime of Partition," in *Notes,* p. 119.

5. The Malay Novels

1. The phrase is Kipling's. See "The White Man's Burden," in *Rudyard Kipling's Verse,* p. 321.

2. Joseph Conrad, *Almayer's Folly* (1895), p. ix. Subsequent references to this edition appear in the text.

3. Conrad, *Nigger of the "Narcissus,"* p. xvi.

4. Adorno, *Authoritarian Personality,* p. 617.

5. Joseph Conrad, *An Outcast of the Islands* (1896), pp. 3–4. Subsequent references to this edition appear in the text.

6. See Thomas Moser, *Joseph Conrad: Achievement and Decline* (Hamden, Conn.: Archon Books, 1966), pp. 50–130.

7. Joseph Conrad, *The Rescue* (1920), p. 367. Subsequent references to this edition appear in the text.

8. Fleishman, *Conrad's Politics,* p. 89.

9. Joseph Conrad, *Lord Jim,* ed. Thomas C. Moser (1900; reprint ed., New York: W. W. Norton, 1968), p. 199. Subsequent references to this edition appear in the text.

10. Albert J. Guerard, *Conrad the Novelist* (1958; reprint ed., New York: Atheneum, 1967).

11. Ibid., p. 161.

12. Raskin, *Mythology.*

13. Ibid., p. 164.

14. V. I. Lenin, *Imperialism: The Highest Stage of Capitalism* (1917; reprint ed., Peking: Foreign Language Press, 1970), p. 101. Mannoni, *Prospero,* p. 32.

6. The Heart of Darkness

1. Conrad, *Heart of Darkness,* p. 11. Subsequent references to this edition appear in the text.

2. Quoted in Baines, *Joseph Conrad,* p. 119.

3. Guerard, *Conrad the Novelist,* pp. 36, 39. Fleishman, *Conrad's Politics,* p. 90. Meyer, *Conrad,* p. 157.

4. Meyer, *Conrad,* pp. 156, 158.

5. Mannoni, *Prospero.*

6. Wayne Booth, *Modern Dogma and the Rhetoric of Assent* (Chicago: University of Chicago Press, 1974).

7. Mannoni, *Prospero,* p. 97.

8. Karl Mannheim, *Ideology and Utopia,* trans. Louis Wirth and Edward Shils (1936; reprint ed., New York: Harcourt, Brace and World, n.d.), pp. 39, 41.

9. Ibid., pp. 259–260.

10. Ibid., p. 47.

11. Joseph Conrad, "An Outpost of Progress," in *Tales of Unrest* (1898), p. 89.

12. See Peter Berger and Thomas Luckmann, *The Social Construction of Reality* (1966; reprint ed., Garden City, N.Y.: Doubleday, Anchor Books, 1967), p. 21.

13. Bruce Johnson, *Conrad's Models of Mind* (Minneapolis, Minn.: University of Minnesota Press, 1971), p. 74.

14. F. R. Leavis, *The Great Tradition* (1948; reprint ed., New York: New York University Press, 1967), p. 177.

15. Joseph Conrad, "Books," in *Notes,* p. 8.

16. Mannheim, *Ideology and Utopia,* p. 47.

7. *Nostromo*

1. Joseph Conrad, *Nostromo* (1904), p. 77. Subsequent references to this edition appear in the text.

2. Stanley J. and Barbara H. Stein, *The Colonial Heritage of Latin America* (New York: Oxford University Press, 1970), p. 161.

3. Orlando Fals Borda, *Subversion and Social Change in Latin America,* trans. Jacqueline Skiles (New York: Columbia University Press, 1969), p. 72.

4. Ibid., p. 78.

5. Ibid., p. 86.

6. Stein and Stein, *Heritage of Latin America,* p. 177.

7. Bolívar to General Juan Jose Flores, November 9, 1830, in *The Liberator, Simon Bolivar,* ed. David Bushnell (New York: Alfred A. Knopf, 1970), p. 86.

8. T. S. Eliot, "Kipling Redivivus," *Athenaeum,* 4645 (May 9, 1919); reprinted in Roger Green, ed., *Kipling: The Critical Heritage* (London: Routledge and Kegan Paul, 1971), p. 324.

Conclusion

1. Conrad, *Heart of Darkness,* p. 50.

INDEX

Adorno, T. W., 10, 103
Almayer's Folly (1895), 99–107, 120–121
"At the End of the Passage" (1980), 32,
    35–36, 41
Authoritarian psychology: Kipling and, 9,
    10, 17, 20, 21, 29, 49, 81, 169; Conrad
    and, 107–114, 170
"Autocracy and War" (1905), 96

"Baa Baa, Black Sheep" (1888), 12–14, 31,
    59, 78
"Beyond the Pale" (1888), 45–48

Capitalism, Conrad's vision of, 94–96,
    154–161
Colonized peoples, Conrad's vision of,
    89, 99–107, 114, 129–130, 135, 137–143
Conrad, Joseph: childhood, 82–87; im-
    perial experiences of, 82–88, 91, 92; as
    imperial artist, 84–87, 93–94, 99–100
Cornell, Louis, 47

Fleishman, Avrom, 2, 86–87, 95–96, 115,
    132
Freud, Sigmund, 146–147
Fromm, Erich, 10, 20

"Galley-Slave, The" (1890), 26–28
Guerard, Albert J., 121, 132

"Head of the District, The" (1890), 24–25
Heart of Darkness (1902), 1, 3, 89–90, 92,
    105, 131–154, 155

"His Chance in Life" (1887), 51–54

Imperial service elite: Kipling's place in,
    1, 9–18; educational program of, 4,
    18–19, 31–33; Kipling's vision of, 5, 18,
    23–29, 30–31; Kipling's program for,
    56–81
Imperial soldier, Kipling's vision of,
    18–21, 42–45
Imperialism: Kipling's program for, 5,
    28–29, 56–58, 64; Kipling's vision of,
    5, 31–33, 34, 85, 92, 98, 107–108,
    112–113; Conrad's vision of, 5, 87–91,
    94–97, 98–99, 107, 120–121, 125, 145,
    153–154, 167, 168–170
Indians, Kipling's vision of, 23–25, 45,
    50–55, 112–113

Johnson, Bruce, 148
"Judgment of Dungara, The" (1888),
    25–26
Jungle Book, The (1894), 33, 56, 59–
    63, 70, 72

Kim (1901), 33, 56, 58, 70–81
Kinkead-Weekes, Mark, 70, 77–78
Kipling, Rudyard: as imperial artist,
    6–7, 30–31, 45–55, 58; childhood,
    9–16, in India, 16–18, 46

Latin America, Conrad's vision of,
    155–167
Leavis, F. R., 149

181